Become a top fact-fetcher with CGP!

Quick question — do you own CGP's
Knowledge Organiser for AQA GCSE Biology?

You do? Great! Now you can use this Knowledge Retriever
to check you've really remembered all the crucial facts.

There are two memory tests for each topic, plus mixed quiz questions
to make extra sure it's all stuck in your brain. Enjoy.

CGP — still the best! ☺

Our sole aim here at CGP is to produce the highest quality books —
carefully written, immaculately presented and dangerously close to being funny.

Then we work our socks off to get them out to you
— at the cheapest possible prices.

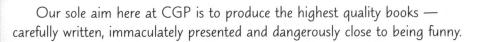

Contents

How to Use This Book..................................2

Working Scientifically

The Scientific Method..............................3

Designing & Performing Experiments..........5

Presenting Data...7

Conclusions, Evaluations and Units...............9

Mixed Practice Quizzes............................11

Topic 1 — Cell Biology

Cells...13

Cell Division...15

Cell Specialisation and Stem Cells...............17

Transport in Cells.....................................19

Exchanging Substances............................21

Mixed Practice Quizzes............................23

Topic 2 — Organisation

Cell Organisation and Enzymes..................25

The Lungs and the Heart...........................27

Blood Vessels and Blood...........................29

Cardiovascular Disease.............................31

Mixed Practice Quizzes............................33

Health and Disease..................................35

Risk Factors for Diseases and Cancer..........37

Plant Cell Organisation.............................39

Transpiration...41

Mixed Practice Quizzes............................43

Topic 3 — Infection and Response

Communicable Disease.............................45

Fighting Disease......................................47

Mixed Practice Quizzes............................49

Drugs..51

Monoclonal Antibodies.............................53

Plant Diseases and Defences.....................55

Mixed Practice Quizzes............................57

Topic 4 — Bioenergetics

Photosynthesis..59

Respiration..61

Metabolism and Exercise..........................63

Mixed Practice Quizzes............................65

Topic 5 — Homeostasis and Response

Homeostasis and the Nervous System......67

Synapses, Reflexes and the Brain...............69

The Eye...71

Mixed Practice Quizzes............................73

Body Temperature and Hormones...............75

Blood Glucose and Hormones....................77

Waste Substances and the Kidneys.............79

Mixed Practice Quizzes............................81

Puberty and the Menstrual Cycle................83

Controlling Fertility..................................85

Plant Hormones.......................................87

Mixed Practice Quizzes............................89

Topic 6 — Inheritance, Variation and Evolution

DNA 91

DNA, Proteins and Mutations 93

Reproduction 95

Mixed Practice Quizzes 97

Genetic Diagrams 99

Inherited Disorders 101

Developments in Genetics & Variation .. 103

Evolution and Speciation 105

Mixed Practice Quizzes 107

Uses of Genetics 109

Fossils and Antibiotic Resistance 111

Classification and Extinction 113

Mixed Practice Quizzes 115

Topic 7 — Ecology

Basics of Ecology 117

Food Chains & Environmental Change .. 119

Cycling of Materials 121

Decay and Biodiversity 123

Mixed Practice Quizzes 125

Human Effects on Ecosystems 127

Maintaining Ecosystems 129

Trophic Levels 131

Food Security and Biotechnology 133

Mixed Practice Quizzes 135

Required Practicals

Required Practicals 1 137

Required Practicals 2 139

Required Practicals 3 141

Required Practicals 4 143

Required Practicals 5 145

Required Practicals 6 147

Mixed Practice Quizzes 149

Practical Skills

Measuring and Sampling 151

Practical Techniques 153

Techniques and Results 155

Mixed Practice Quizzes 157

Published by CGP.
From original material by Richard Parsons.

Editors: Luke Bennett, Ellen Burton, Sam Mann, Rachael Rogers.
Contributors: Paddy Gannon.

ISBN: 978 1 78908 493 1

With thanks to Emily Smith for the copyright research.

Printed by Elanders Ltd, Newcastle upon Tyne.
Clipart from Corel®
Illustrations by: Sandy Gardner Artist, email sandy@sandygardner.co.uk

Text, design, layout and original illustrations © Coordination Group Publications Ltd (CGP) 2020
All rights reserved.

How to Use This Book

Every page in this book has a matching page in the GCSE Biology **Knowledge Organiser**.
Before using this book, try to **memorise** everything on a Knowledge Organiser page.
Then follow these **seven steps** to see how much knowledge you're able to retrieve...

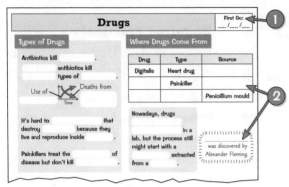

1 In this book, there are two versions
of each page. Find the **'First Go'** of
the page you've tried to memorise,
and write the **date** at the top.

2 Use what you've learned from the
Knowledge Organiser to **fill in**
any dotted lines or white spaces.

⌇⎪⎪⎪⎪⎪⎪⎪⎪⎪⎪⎪⎪⎪⎪⎪⎪⎪⎪⎪⎪⎪⎪⎪⎪⎪⎪⎪⎪⎪⌇
You may need to draw, complete
or add labels to diagrams too.
⌇⎪⎪⎪⎪⎪⎪⎪⎪⎪⎪⎪⎪⎪⎪⎪⎪⎪⎪⎪⎪⎪⎪⎪⎪⎪⎪⎪⌇

3 Use the Knowledge Organiser to **check your work**.
Use a **different coloured pen** to write in anything you missed or that wasn't quite right.
This lets you see clearly what you **know** and what you **don't know**.

4 After doing the First Go page, **wait a few days**. This is important because **spacing out**
your retrieval practice helps you to remember things better.

5 Now do the **Second Go** page.
⌇⎪⎪⎪⎪⎪⎪⎪⎪⎪⎪⎪⎪⎪⎪⎪⎪⎪⎪⎪⎪⎪⎪⎪⌇
The Second Go page is harder
— it has more things missing.
⌇⎪⎪⎪⎪⎪⎪⎪⎪⎪⎪⎪⎪⎪⎪⎪⎪⎪⎪⎪⎪⎪⌇

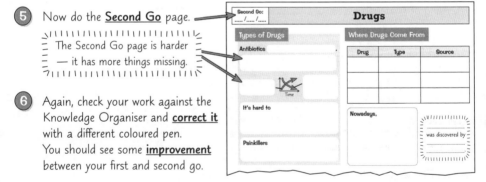

6 Again, check your work against the
Knowledge Organiser and **correct it**
with a different coloured pen.
You should see some **improvement**
between your first and second go.

7 **Wait** another few days, then try recreating the whole Knowledge Organiser page on a
blank piece of paper. If you can do this, you'll know you've **really learned it**.

There are also **Mixed Practice Quizzes** dotted throughout the book:
• The quizzes come in sets of four. They test a mix of content from the previous few pages.
• Do each quiz on a different day — write the date you do each one at the top of the quiz.
• Tick the questions you get right and record your score in the box at the end.

The Scientific Method

First Go:
..... /..... /.....

Developing Theories

Come up with [ ]

↓

Test [ ]

↓

Evidence is [ ]

↓

If all evidence backs up hypothesis, it becomes an [ ].

HYPOTHESIS — a possible explanation for an [ ].

PEER REVIEW — when [ ] check results and explanations before they're [ ].

Accepted theories can still [ ] as more evidence is found, e.g. inheritance and genetics:

characteristics are determined by "hereditary units" → "units" are genes on chromosomes → structure of DNA shows how genes work

Models

REPRESENTATIONAL MODELS — a simplified [ ] or [ ] of the real system, e.g. lock and key model of enzyme action:

enzyme — active site — substrate → fit like lock and key

Models help scientists explain [ ] and make [ ].

COMPUTATIONAL MODELS — computers are used to simulate [ ].

Issues in Science

Scientific developments can create four issues:

1. Economic — e.g. beneficial technology, like [ ], may be too [ ] to use.

2. Environmental — e.g. new technology could [ ] the natural environment.

3. [ ] — decisions based on [ ] can affect society, e.g. taxing alcohol to reduce health problems.

4. [ ] — some decisions affect [ ], e.g. a person may not want a wind farm being built near to their home.

[ ] on scientific developments may be oversimplified, inaccurate or [ ].

Hazard and Risk

HAZARD — something that could potentially [ ].

RISK — the [ ] that a [ ] will cause harm.

Hazards associated with biology experiments include:

• Some microorganisms can [ ].

• [ ] chemicals (e.g. flammable ethanol).

• [ ] electrical equipment can give you a [ ].

The [ ] of the harm and the [ ] of it happening both need consideration.

 ✓ ✓ ✓

The Scientific Method

Developing Theories

Come up with _____

↓

_____

↓

_____

↓

If all evidence _____

HYPOTHESIS —

PEER REVIEW —

Accepted theories can still

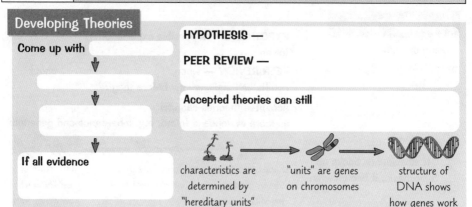

characteristics are determined by "hereditary units" → "units" are genes on chromosomes → structure of DNA shows how genes work

Models

REPRESENTATIONAL MODELS —

enzyme active site substrate → fit like lock and key

Models help _____

COMPUTATIONAL MODELS — computers are _____

Issues in Science

Scientific developments can create four issues:

1 Economic — e.g. beneficial technology,

2 Environmental — e.g. new technology

3 Social — decisions based on research can

4 Personal — some decisions affect

Media reports on scientific developments may be

Hazard and Risk

HAZARD —

RISK —

Hazards associated with biology experiments include:

• Some microorganisms

• Hazardous

• Faulty electrical

The seriousness of the _____ and the

 ☑ ☑ ☑

Designing & Performing Experiments

Collecting Data

	Data should be...
REPEATABLE	Same person gets .... after repeating experiment using the same ....
REPRODUCIBLE	Similar results can be achieved by ...., or by using a .... method or piece of equipment.
	Results are close to the true answer.
PRECISE	All data is ....

Reliable data is .... and ....

.... are repeatable and reproducible and answer ....

Fair Tests

INDEPENDENT VARIABLE	Variable that you ....
DEPENDENT VARIABLE	
.... VARIABLE	Variable that is kept the same.
CONTROL EXPERIMENT	An experiment kept under the .... as the rest of the .... without anything being done to it.
FAIR TEST	An experiment where only the .... changes, whilst all other variables are ....

Control experiments are carried out when .... can't be ....

Four Things to Look Out For

1. **RANDOM ERRORS** — .... caused by things like .... in measuring.

2. **SYSTEMATIC ERRORS** — measurements that are .... by the .... each time.

3. **ZERO ERRORS** — .... that are caused by using a piece of equipment that isn't ....

4. **ANOMALOUS RESULTS** — results that don't fit with the ....

Anomalous results can be ignored if you know ....

Processing Data

Calculate the .... — .... all data values and divide by ....

UNCERTAINTY — the amount by which a given result may .... from the ....

$$............... = \frac{range}{2}$$

.... value minus .... value

In any calculation, you should .... to the lowest number of significant figures (s.f.) given.

Working Scientifically

Second Go: ...../...../.....	**Designing & Performing Experiments**

Collecting Data

	Data should be...	
REPEATABLE	Same person gets	....
REPRODUCIBLE	Similar results can be achieved by someone else,	....
PRECISE	Results are	....

Fair Tests

INDEPENDENT VARIABLE	
DEPENDENT VARIABLE	
CONTROL VARIABLE	
CONTROL EXPERIMENT	An experiment kept
FAIR TEST	An experiment where

Control experiments are carried out ....

Four Things to Look Out For

1 RANDOM ERRORS —

2 SYSTEMATIC ERRORS —

3 ZERO ERRORS —

4 ANOMALOUS RESULTS —

Anomalous results ....

Processing Data

Calculate the mean —

UNCERTAINTY —

$= \dfrac{\text{range}}{\boxed{}}$

In any calculation, ...

  ✓ ✓ ✓

Presenting Data

Bar Charts

Bar charts are used when independent variable is _____ .

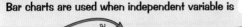

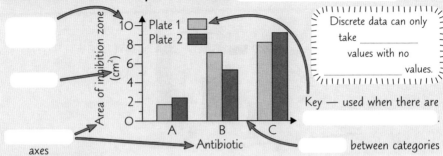

Discrete data can only take _____ values with no _____ values.

Key — used when there are _____ .

_____ axes

_____ between categories

Plotting Graphs

Graphs are used when both variables are _____ .

Continuous data — can take any numerical value _____ .

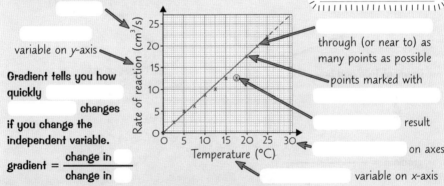

_____ variable on y-axis

Gradient tells you how quickly _____ changes if you change the independent variable.

$$\text{gradient} = \frac{\text{change in } \boxed{}}{\text{change in } \boxed{}}$$

_____ through (or near to) as many points as possible

points marked with _____

_____ result

_____ on axes

_____ variable on x-axis

Three Types of Correlation Between Variables

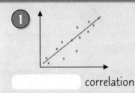

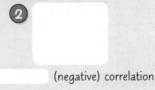

_____ correlation

_____ (negative) correlation

_____ correlation

Possible reasons for a correlation:

Chance — correlation might be a _____ .

Third variable — another _____ links the _____ .

Cause — if every other variable that could affect the result is _____ , you can conclude that changing one variable causes the _____ .

Working Scientifically

Presenting Data

Bar Charts

Bar charts are

Discrete data can only take

Plate 1
Plate 2

Key —

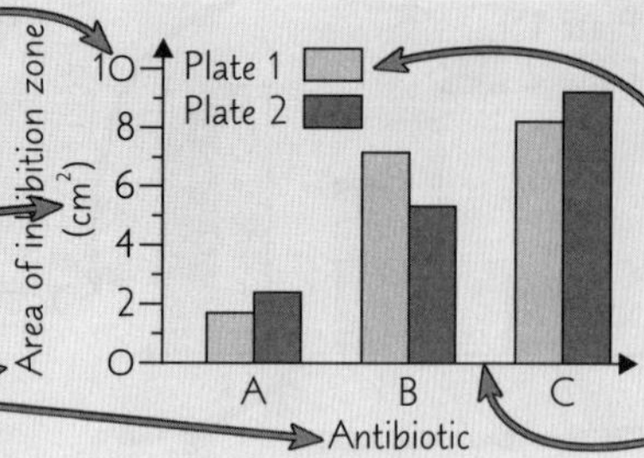

Area of inhibition zone (cm²)

10
8
6
4
2
0

A   B   C

Antibiotic

Plotting Graphs

Continuous data —

Graphs are used

line of best fit

Gradient tells you how

points

Rate of reaction (cm³/s)

25
20
15
10
5
0

0   5   10   15   20   25   30

Temperature (°C)

gradient = ————————

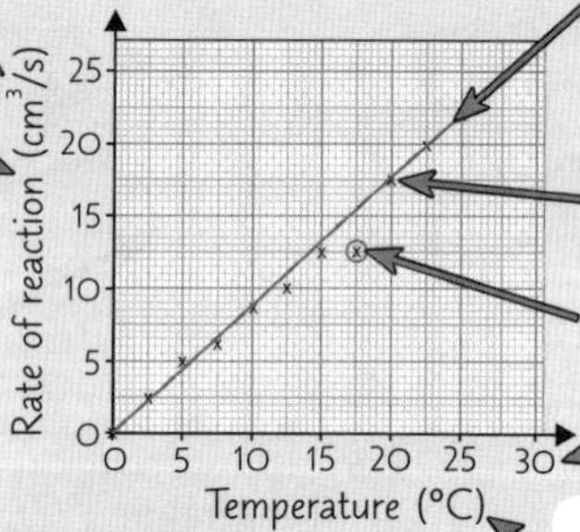

Three Types of Correlation Between Variables

1

2

3

Positive correlation   (negative) correlation   No correlation

Possible reasons for a correlation:

Chance —

Third variable —

Cause —

Working Scientifically

Conclusions, Evaluations and Units

Conclusions

Draw conclusion by [_____] between dependent and independent variables.

↓

Justify conclusion using [_____].

↓

Refer to [_____] and state whether data supports it.

> You can only draw a conclusion from ....
> ....
> — you can't go any further than that.

Evaluations

EVALUATION — a [_____] of the whole investigation.

	Things to consider
Method	• [_____] of method • Control of [_____]
Results	• [_____], accuracy, [_____] and reproducibility of results • Number of [_____] taken • Level of [_____] in the results
Anomalous results	• [_____] of any anomalous results

> You could make more .... based on your conclusion, which you could test in ....

Repeating experiment with [_____] to improve the quality of results will give you more [_____] in your conclusions.

S.I. Units

S.I. BASE UNITS — a set of [_____] that all scientists use.

Quantity	S.I. Unit
mass	kilogram ([___])
length	[___] (m)
[___]	second (s)

Scaling Units

SCALING PREFIX — a word or symbol that goes before a unit to indicate a [_____].

Multiple of unit	Prefix
10^{12}	tera ( )
10^9	giga ( )
10^6	mega ( )
[___]	[___] (k)
	deci (d)
0.01	[___]
0.001	[___]
10^{-6}	[___] (μ)
	nano (n)

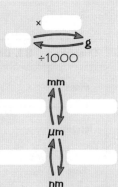

Conclusions, Evaluations and Units

Conclusions

Draw conclusion by

↓

↓

Refer to _____ .

You can only
_____
_____
— you can't go any

Evaluations

EVALUATION — _____ .

	Things to consider
Method	• •
Results	• • Number of • Level of
Anomalous results	•

You could make more
_____
based on your
conclusion, which you
could test in

Repeating experiment with changes to improve

S.I. Units

S.I. BASE UNITS —

Quantity	S.I. Unit
mass	
length	
time	

Scaling Units

SCALING PREFIX — a word or symbol that goes before
_____ .

Multiple of unit	Prefix
10^{12}	
10^9	
10^6	
10^{-6}	
10^{-9}	

g

mm
÷ ⟳ x

nm
÷ ⟳ x

Working Scientifically

 √ √ √

Mixed Practice Quizzes

You've reached the conclusion of this topic. Time to evaluate your knowledge of p.3-10 by working through the following quiz questions methodically. I'll stop now.

Quiz 1

Date: ...... / ...... / ......

1) True or false? Bar charts are often used to display experimental results where the independent variable is discrete.
2) On a graph, does the independent variable go on the x-axis or the y-axis?
3) Give three possible reasons for a correlation between variables.
4) What is meant by 'risk' in an investigation?
5) Why can accepted theories still change over time?
6) Describe how to draw a line of best fit on a graph.
7) What is a control experiment?
8) What are 'random errors' in an experiment?
9) What are anomalous results?
10) What does it mean if the results of an experiment are reproducible?

Total:

Quiz 2

Date: ...... / ...... / ......

1) What are S.I. units?
2) What is a hypothesis?
3) Give three hazards associated with biology experiments.
4) What is meant by the 'uncertainty' of a result?
5) What is a representational model?
6) Would it be better to use a bar chart or a graph to present the results of an experiment in which both variables are continuous?
7) What is an evaluation?
8) What does the gradient of a graph tell you?
9) Give an example of an accepted theory that has changed over time.
10) What does it mean if results are 'valid'?

Total:

Mixed Practice Quizzes

Quiz 3 Date: ...... / ...... / ......

1) What are 'systematic errors' in an experiment?
2) Give two reasons why models are useful for scientists.
3) In an investigation, is the independent variable the variable that you change or the variable that you measure?
4) What does it mean if results are 'accurate'?
5) Give two things you should consider about your method when you're writing an evaluation.
6) When can anomalous results be ignored?
7) Give the S.I. units for: a) mass,   b) length,   c) time.
8) What is peer review?
9) Give three types of correlation that can be shown between variables.
10) Give three things you should include when writing a conclusion.

Total:

Quiz 4 Date: ...... / ...... / ......

1) What is a control variable?
2) How do you convert a value from mm to μm?
3) Give four types of issues scientific developments can create.
4) What does it mean if data is described as 'precise'?
5) If the same person can get the same results using the same method and equipment, is the data considered repeatable or reproducible?
6) Give three features of a bar chart.
7) How is the mean of a set of results calculated?
8) How do you calculate the gradient of a line on a graph?
9) Give one issue related to media reports about scientific developments.
10) How do you calculate the uncertainty of a mean result?

Total:

Cells

First Go:
..... /..... /.....

Eukaryotic Cells

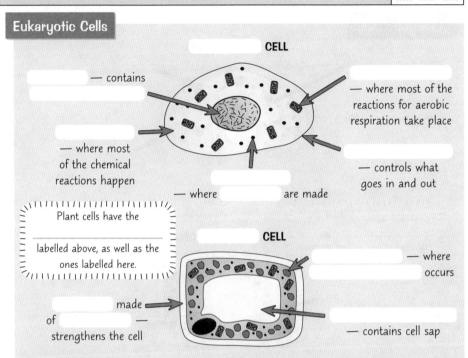

_____ CELL

_____ — contains

— where most
of the chemical
reactions happen

— where _____ are made

— where most of the
reactions for aerobic
respiration take place

— controls what
goes in and out

Plant cells have the
....
labelled above, as well as the
ones labelled here.

_____ CELL

— where
occurs

_____ made —
of _____ —
strengthens the cell

— contains cell sap

Prokaryotic Cells

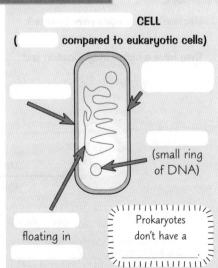

_____ CELL

(_____ compared to eukaryotic cells)

_____

(small ring
of DNA)

floating in
_____

Prokaryotes
don't have a
....

Microscopy

_____ microscopes were
invented later than _____ microscopes.
They have a higher _____
and _____ than _____
microscopes — they let us see
_____ in more detail,
meaning we can understand
_____ better now.

$$_____ = \frac{\text{image size}}{\text{real size}}$$

Use _____ to
write really _____ .
E.g. 0.0045 = 4.5 × 10⁻³

Topic 1 — Cell Biology

Second Go:
..... /..... /.....

Cells

Eukaryotic Cells

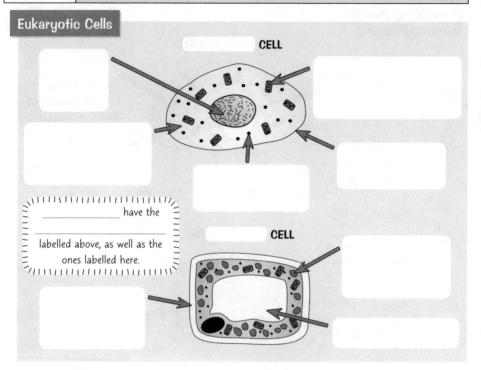

_____ CELL

_____ have the
_____
labelled above, as well as the
ones labelled here.

_____ CELL

Prokaryotic Cells

_____ CELL
(_____ compared to
_____)

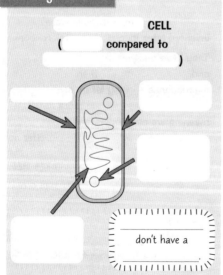

don't have a
_____.

Microscopy

Electron microscopes were invented

They have a higher magnification and

$$= \frac{\text{size}}{\text{size}}$$

Use _____ to
_____.
E.g. 0.0045 = _____

Cell Division

Chromosomes and the Cell Cycle

CHROMOSOMES — coiled up lengths of _____ , which carry _____ .
They're found in the _____ , and they're normally in _____ .

CELL CYCLE — a series of stages in which _____ to produce _____ .

Before _____ , it does three things:

1 _____ .

2 Increases the amount of _____ ,
e.g. _____ and _____ .

3 _____ its DNA.

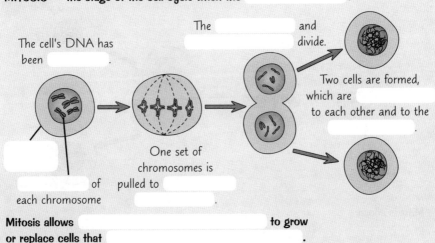

The
....
....

and

mitosis

Mitosis

MITOSIS — the stage of the cell cycle when the _____ .

The cell's DNA has been _____ .

The _____ and _____ divide.

Two cells are formed, which are _____ to each other and to the _____

_____ of each chromosome

One set of chromosomes is pulled to _____ .

Mitosis allows _____ to grow or replace cells that _____ .

Binary Fission

BINARY FISSION — the simple cell division process by which _____ . It can happen as often as _____ if there are enough _____ and the _____ .

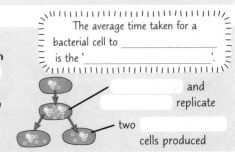

The average time taken for a bacterial cell to _____ is the ' _____ '.

_____ and _____ replicate

two _____ cells produced

Topic 1 — Cell Biology

Cell Division

Chromosomes and the Cell Cycle

CHROMOSOMES — _____ .

They're found _____

CELL CYCLE — _____ .

Before _____ , it does three things:

1 _____

2 _____

3 _____

and

The
....
....

Mitosis

MITOSIS — _____ .

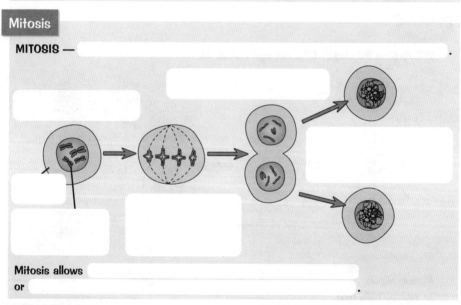

Mitosis allows _____

or _____ .

Binary Fission

BINARY FISSION —

It can happen

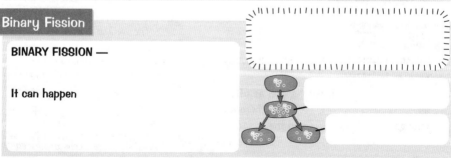

Cell Specialisation and Stem Cells

Cell Differentiation

DIFFERENTIATION — the process by which a [_____]
to become [_____].

In most [_____], the ability to differentiate is lost at an
[_____], but many [_____] never lose this ability.

Five Types of Specialised Cells

1 Sperm cell — [_____]
[_____] tail and streamlined
[_____] for swimming to the [_____].

2 Nerve cell — [_____]

Long to cover a [_____],
and [_____] to form a
[_____].

3 Xylem and phloem — [_____] cells are hollow and [_____]
[_____] cells have few subcellular structures,
so substances can [_____].

4 Muscle cell — [_____]
Long so they have
[_____], and lots of
mitochondria for [_____].

5 Root hair cell — [_____]

Large surface area for
[_____] and
[_____] from the soil.

Stem Cells

STEM CELLS — [_____]
[_____], which can divide to
produce lots more [_____],
and can [_____]
into many other types of cell.

Stem cells from...	Can become...
adult bone marrow	
	any kind of human cell
plant meristem	

Stem cells can be [_____] and made to differentiate into [_____] cells:

Uses in medicine	Uses in plants
E.g. stem cells could produce [_____] to treat [_____], or insulin-producing cells to treat [_____].	Produce [_____] of whole plants
In [_____], an embryo could be made with the [_____] as the patient — then stem cells used from the embryo wouldn't be rejected by the patient.	e.g. to grow more plants of a rare species, or clone crops with [_____].

Risk: stem cells from the lab could [_____], which could get transferred to the [_____].

18

Cell Differentiation

DIFFERENTIATION —

In most _____ , the ability to _____
_____ , but many _____ .

Five Types of Specialised Cells

1 Sperm cell —

2 Nerve cell —

Long to cover

3 Xylem and phloem —

Xylem cells are hollow and phloem cells

4 Muscle cell —

Long so they have

5 Root hair cell —

Large surface area

Stem Cells

STEM CELLS —

Stem cells from...	Can become...

Stem cells can be _____ and _____ cells:

Uses in medicine:	Uses in plants:

Risk: stem cells from the lab could _____ , which _____ .

Transport in Cells

Diffusion

DIFFUSION — the spreading out of _____ from an area of _____ to an area of _____ .

Only very _____ (e.g. oxygen, glucose) can diffuse through _____ .

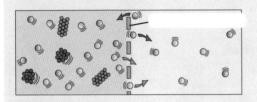

These three factors _____ the rate of diffusion across a _____ :

1. A high _____ (e.g. loads of the _____ on one side and hardly any on the other).

2. _____

3. A _____ surface area.

Osmosis

OSMOSIS — the movement of _____ molecules across a _____ from a region of _____ to a region of _____ .

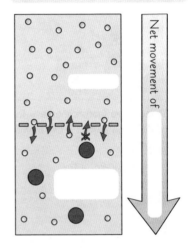

Net movement of _____

Active Transport

ACTIVE TRANSPORT — the _____ of a substance against the _____ . Unlike diffusion and osmosis, it requires _____ . It allows...

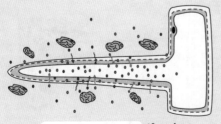

... _____ (for plant growth) to be absorbed from the soil into _____ .

glucose

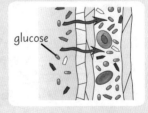

... _____ (for cell respiration) to be absorbed into the _____ from the _____ .

 ☑ ☑ ☑

Transport in Cells

Diffusion

DIFFUSION —

Only

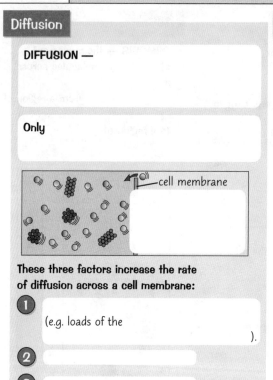

cell membrane

These three factors increase the rate
of diffusion across a cell membrane:

1

(e.g. loads of the

).

2

3

Osmosis

OSMOSIS —

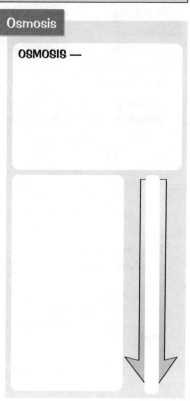

Active Transport

ACTIVE TRANSPORT —

It allows...

... mineral ions

...

from the gut.

Exchanging Substances

Surface Area to Volume Ratio

Single-celled organism

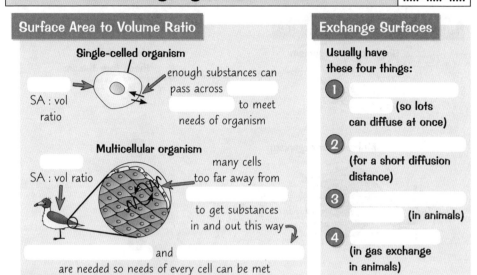

SA : vol ratio

enough substances can pass across

to meet needs of organism

Multicellular organism

SA : vol ratio

many cells too far away from

to get substances in and out this way

and

are needed so needs of every cell can be met

Exchange Surfaces

Usually have these four things:

1

(so lots can diffuse at once)

2

(for a short diffusion distance)

3

(in animals)

4

(in gas exchange in animals)

Four Organs Adapted for Exchange

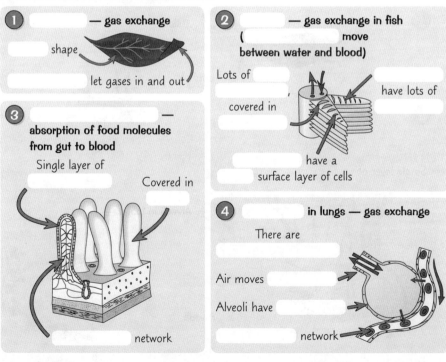

1 — gas exchange

shape

let gases in and out

2 — gas exchange in fish
(move between water and blood)

Lots of

covered in

have lots of

have a surface layer of cells

3 —
absorption of food molecules from gut to blood

Single layer of

Covered in

network

4 in lungs — gas exchange

There are

Air moves

Alveoli have

network

22

Second Go: ..... /..... /.....	# Exchanging Substances

Surface Area to Volume Ratio

Single-celled organism

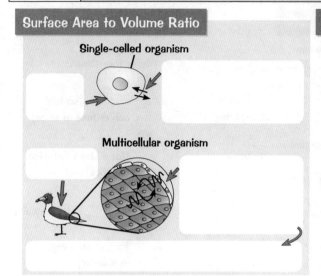

Multicellular organism

Exchange Surfaces

Usually have these four things:

1

2

3

4

Four Organs Adapted for Exchange

1

in and out

2 Gills —

Lots of

3

Single layer of

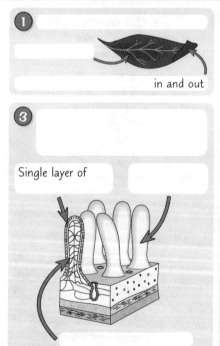

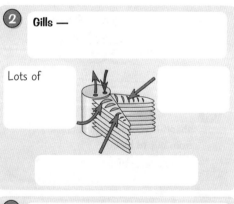

4 Alveoli in lungs —

Alveoli

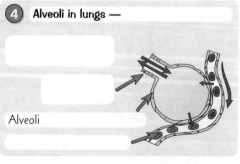

Topic 1 — Cell Biology

Mixed Practice Quizzes

That's your lot for this topic. Before you get carried away with your cell-ebrations, have a go at these quizzes based on p.13-22 to see how much you've learnt.

Quiz 1   Date: ...... / ...... / ......

1) What does a cell's nucleus contain?
2) Give three factors that increase the rate of diffusion.
3) Which process is used to absorb mineral ions from the soil into a plant's root hair cells?
4) Give three ways in which fish gills are adapted for gas exchange.
5) What is the function of a cell membrane?
6) What are plant cell walls made from?
7) What is binary fission?
8) What is cell differentiation?
9) True or false? Electron microscopes were invented before light microscopes.
10) What is the cell cycle?

Total:

Quiz 2   Date: ...... / ...... / ......

1) What is diffusion?
2) Give three things a cell does before it divides by mitosis.
3) In which subcellular structure are proteins made?
4) During mitosis, where do the two sets of chromosomes move to before a cell divides?
5) What is active transport?
6) What do you divide the size of an image by to find its magnification?
7) Why do many organisms need exchange surfaces and transport systems?
8) Where does photosynthesis occur in plant cells?
9) Give two uses of plant stem cells.
10) How often can bacterial cells replicate if there are enough nutrients available and the temperature is suitable?

Total:

Topic 1 — Cell Biology

Mixed Practice Quizzes

Quiz 3

Date: ...... / ...... / ......

1) What is a chromosome?
2) How are nerve cells specialised for their function?
3) Where is DNA found in a bacterial cell?
4) Give two differences between diffusion and active transport.
5) True or false? A stem cell taken from adult bone marrow can become any kind of human cell.
6) What does the permanent vacuole of a plant cell contain?
7) Give one condition that treatment with stem cells could potentially help.
8) Where in a cell do most chemical reactions take place?
9) During which stage of the cell cycle do cells divide?
10) Give four common characteristics of exchange surfaces.

Total:

Quiz 4

Date: ...... / ...... / ......

1) What are stem cells?
2) What is osmosis?
3) Which cells are bigger: eukaryotic cells or prokaryotic cells?
4) Give a potential risk of using stem cells in medicine.
5) Where in a cell do most of the chemical reactions for aerobic respiration take place?
6) How many identical cells are formed from a single parent cell during mitosis?
7) How have electron microscopes allowed scientists to better understand subcellular structures?
8) True or false? Most animal cells lose the ability to differentiate at an early stage.
9) Which organisms have larger surface area to volume ratios: single-celled organisms or multicellular organisms?
10) Give four ways lungs are adapted for gas exchange.

Total:

Cell Organisation and Enzymes

First Go:
..... /..... /.....

Cell Organisation

_____ — a basic building block that all living organisms have.

⬇

TISSUE —

⬇

_____ — a group of different _____ that work together.

⬇

ORGAN SYSTEM —

Organ systems work together to make entire _____.

Enzymes

Enzymes _____ (speed up) chemical reactions. Each enzyme only _____ one specific reaction because of the unique shape of its _____.

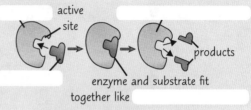

active site

products

enzyme and substrate fit together like _____

_____ temperatures and high and low pHs change the shape of _____ so the enzyme no longer works.

Reaction rate

_____ temp.

Temp.

0 °C   45 °C

enzyme _____

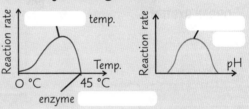

Reaction rate

pH

Digestion

_____ break BIG molecules down into smaller, soluble ones. These can pass through the walls of the digestive system and be _____.

Enzyme	Breaks down...	Into...	Produced in the...
_____ (a carbohydrase)	_____	other sugars	_____, small intestine, _____
_____	protein	_____ acids	_____, intestine, pancreas
lipase	_____	_____, fatty acids	_____, pancreas

The products of digestion can be used to make new _____.

Bile speeds up digestion in two ways:

1 It makes conditions _____ so enzymes in the _____ work better.

2 It _____ so there's a larger surface area for _____ to work on.

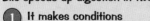

Bile is made in the _____ and stored in the _____.

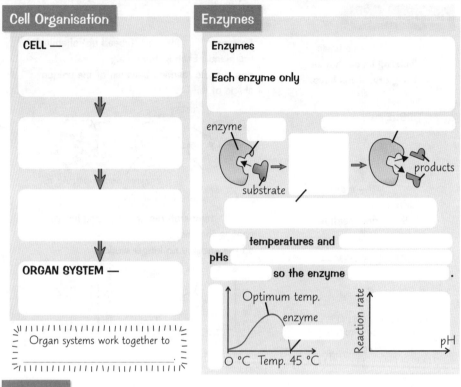

Second Go:
...../...../.....

Cell Organisation and Enzymes

Cell Organisation

CELL —

⬇

⬇

⬇

ORGAN SYSTEM —

Organ systems work together to
....

Enzymes

Enzymes

Each enzyme only

enzyme

substrate → products

temperatures and pHs

so the enzyme .

Optimum temp.

enzyme

0 °C   Temp. 45 °C

Reaction rate

pH

Digestion

Digestive enzymes .

These can pass through

.

Enzyme	Breaks down...	Into...	Produced in the...
amylase (a carbohydrase)			
	protein		
		glycerol, fatty acids	

The .... of digestion can be used ....

Bile speeds up digestion in two ways:

1

2

Bile is

The Lungs and the Heart

The Lungs

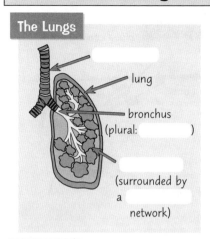

lung

bronchus
(plural:)

(surrounded by
a
network)

Gas Exchange

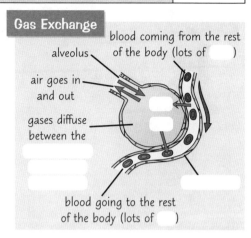

blood coming from the rest
of the body (lots of)

alveolus

air goes in
and out

gases diffuse
between the

blood going to the rest
of the body (lots of)

The Heart

The   system is made up of the heart (a pumping organ), blood vessels and blood. Humans have a   (two circuits):

Circuit 1 — heart (ventricle) ➡ lungs ⇨

Circuit 2 — heart (ventricle) ⇨   ➡ heart

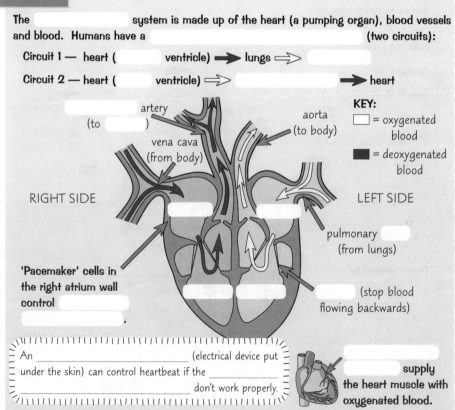

artery
(to   )

vena cava
(from body)

aorta
(to body)

KEY:
☐ = oxygenated
blood
■ = deoxygenated
blood

RIGHT SIDE

LEFT SIDE

pulmonary
(from lungs)

'Pacemaker' cells in
the right atrium wall
control   .

(stop blood
flowing backwards)

An   (electrical device put
under the skin) can control heartbeat if the
                    don't work properly.

                    supply
the heart muscle with
oxygenated blood.

Topic 2 — Organisation

The Lungs and the Heart

The Lungs

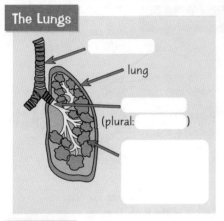

lung

(plural:)

Gas Exchange

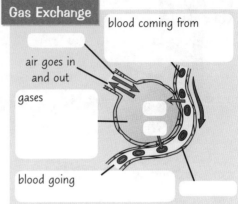

blood coming from

air goes in
and out

gases

blood going

The Heart

The circulatory system

Humans have

Circuit 1 —

Circuit 2 —

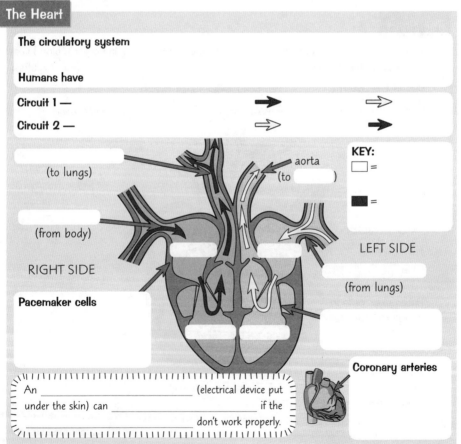

(to lungs)

aorta

(to)

KEY:

☐ =

■ =

(from body)

LEFT SIDE

RIGHT SIDE

(from lungs)

Pacemaker cells

Coronary arteries

An _____ (electrical device put
under the skin) can _____ if the
_____ don't work properly.

 ✓ ✓ ✓

Blood Vessels and Blood

Three Types of Blood Vessel

1 _____ carry blood away from the heart.

thick muscle and elastic layers because blood pressure is _____

2 _____ carry blood close to body cells to exchange substances.

thin, _____ walls to allow substances to _____ in and out easily

3 _____ carry blood back to the heart.

_____ inside stop blood flowing backwards

thinner walls than _____ because blood pressure is _____

$$\text{rate of blood flow} = \frac{\text{volume of blood}}{\text{..................}}$$

Four Blood Components

Blood is a _____ .

Component	Function	Description
1 _____ blood cells	Carry _____ around the body.	no _____ so more room for _____ _____ shape = big surface area = lots of _____ absorbed 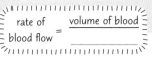 contains _____ , which binds to _____
2 _____ blood cells	Defend against _____ .	_____ → phagocytosis → antitoxins → _____
3 Platelets	Help blood to _____ .	fragments of _____ →
4 _____	Carries _____ in the blood.	amino acids, hormones, red blood cells, urea, glucose, antibodies, antitoxins, white blood cells, proteins, platelets, CO_2 liquid

Blood Vessels and Blood

Three Types of Blood Vessel

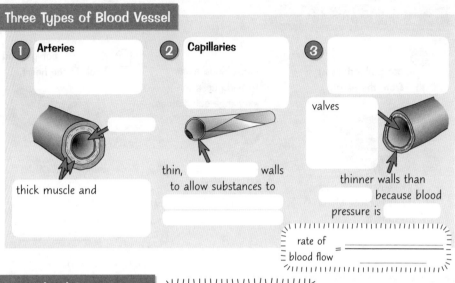

1 Arteries

2 Capillaries

3

valves

thick muscle and

thin, _____ walls
to allow substances to

thinner walls than
_____ because blood
pressure is _____

$$\text{rate of blood flow} = \frac{\rule{3cm}{0.4pt}}{\rule{3cm}{0.4pt}}$$

Four Blood Components

Component	Function	Description
1		no _____ so more room for _____ contains _____	_____ = big surface area = _____
2		
3 Platelets		
4		hormones amino acids antibodies urea glucose antitoxins proteins CO_2

Cardiovascular Disease

Coronary Heart Disease

_____ — diseases of the heart or blood vessels, e.g. coronary heart disease:

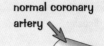

normal coronary artery

coronary artery of someone with coronary heart disease

blood flow is _____ so there's a lack of _____ to the _____ muscle

Five Treatments for Cardiovascular Disease

Treatment	Advantages	Disadvantages
1 Statins	_____ the amount of LDL cholesterol in the blood, which slows down the formation of _____ .	• Need to be taken long-term. • Can have _____ .
2 _____ (tube put in coronary artery) fatty deposit squashed _____	• Keeps coronary arteries open for a long time. • _____ is pretty quick.	• _____ can cause bleeding and infection. • Donor hearts or valves can be _____ .
3 _____ (heart from a donor)	• Can treat heart failure. • Donor hearts work better than _____ .	• Artificial devices can lead to _____ (blood clots in blood vessels).
4 _____	Can be used while waiting for a donor heart or while the heart is _____ .	
5 Replacement heart valves — _____ or _____	Can treat severe valve damage (e.g. stiff valves that don't open properly or _____).	Faulty heart valves stop _____

Topic 2 — Organisation

Cardiovascular Disease

Coronary Heart Disease

CARDIOVASCULAR DISEASES —

normal coronary
artery

coronary artery of someone
with coronary heart disease

Five Treatments for Cardiovascular Disease

Treatment	Advantages	Disadvantages
1 Statins	Reduce the amount of	• •
2	• Keeps coronary arteries •	• Surgery can • Donor hearts or valves can
3 (heart from a donor)	• •	
4 Artificial heart		• Artificial devices can
5		Faulty heart valves ....

Mixed Practice Quizzes

I know you've been turning every page excitedly wondering when the next quizzes were coming... well, the wait is over — time to test yourself on p.25-32.

Quiz 1 Date: ...... / ...... / ......

1) Where in the heart are pacemaker cells found?
2) Define 'organ'.
3) Which enzyme breaks down starch?
4) Which side of the heart receives blood from the lungs?
5) How do stents work as a treatment for coronary heart disease?
6) Why do capillaries have thin, permeable walls?
7) What is the liquid component of blood called?
8) Why is each enzyme only able to catalyse one specific reaction?
9) Name the structures in the lungs where gas exchange takes place.
10) What is the role of digestive enzymes?

Total:

Quiz 2 Date: ...... / ...... / ......

1) Where is bile made? Where is it stored?
2) Which blood vessels supply the heart muscle with oxygenated blood?
3) How do statins help people with cardiovascular diseases?
4) Why don't enzymes work at high temperatures?
5) What does an artificial pacemaker do?
6) Give three places in the body where protease is produced.
7) Explain why there is a lack of oxygen reaching the heart muscle in people with coronary heart disease.
8) How does the structure of arteries make them suited to their function?
9) What do platelets do?
10) Give two advantages of heart transplants.

Total:

Topic 2 — Organisation

Mixed Practice Quizzes

Quiz 3   Date: ...... / ...... / ......

1) Why is the term 'lock and key' used to describe enzyme action?
2) What is the name for the two tubes that the trachea splits into, one of which goes into each lung?
3) Give three examples of things carried in the plasma.
4) What does lipase break lipids down into?
5) List three ways that white blood cells defend against infection.
6) Give two disadvantages of using statins to treat cardiovascular diseases.
7) Which digestive enzyme is produced in the salivary glands, small intestine and pancreas?
8) Describe the role of the pulmonary artery.
9) Which type of blood vessel has valves inside?
10) How does the shape of red blood cells make them adapted for carrying oxygen around the body?

Total:

Quiz 4   Date: ...... / ...... / ......

1) What term describes a group of organs that work together?
2) What is the role of the aorta?
3) Why do arteries have thicker walls than veins?
4) Describe the movement of gases between alveoli and the capillaries that surround them.
5) Define 'tissue'.
6) Which chamber of the heart pumps blood to the lungs?
7) Explain two ways in which bile speeds up digestion.
8) Explain what happens to an enzyme's activity at extreme pHs.
9) Give two possible problems with heart valves that could lead to a person needing replacement valves.
10) Give one disadvantage of donor hearts and valves.

Total:

Health and Disease

Health

HEALTH —

_____ can cause ill health.

These three things can also affect health:

1. _____

2. stress

3. life situation, e.g. _____

Two Types of Disease

1. COMMUNICABLE DISEASE —
a disease that can spread from
_____ or
between _____
_____ .

2. NON-COMMUNICABLE
DISEASE —

Four Ways That Diseases May Interact

	Initial problem	Issue that can be made more likely
1	disorder affecting immune system	_____ diseases
2	infection by certain _____	certain cancers
3	pathogen infection that causes _____	_____ (e.g. rashes or asthma)
4	severe physical health problems	mental health issues (e.g. _____)

Cost of Non-Communicable Diseases

Human cost —

_____ of
people die from non-communicable
diseases each _____ .

Those living with these diseases may
have a poorer quality of life and
_____ .

Financial cost —

_____
_____
costs health organisations
(e.g. the NHS) loads of money.

Those with diseases may not be
able to work, which can affect
_____ as well as
the _____ .

36

Health and Disease

Health

HEALTH —

_____ can cause ill health.

These three things can also affect health:

1
2
3

Two Types of Disease

1 COMMUNICABLE DISEASE —

2

Four Ways That Diseases May Interact

	Initial problem	Issue that can be made more likely
1	disorder affecting	diseases
2	infection by	certain
3		
4	severe problems	

Cost of Non-Communicable Diseases

Human cost —

Financial cost —

Those living with

Those with diseases

Topic 2 — Organisation

Risk Factors for Diseases and Cancer

Five Risk Factors for Non-Communicable Diseases

RISK FACTORS —

1. A lack of _____ and an unhealthy (e.g. _____) diet are linked to cardiovascular disease.

2. Obesity is linked to Type ___ diabetes and cancer of the bowel, liver and _____.

3. Drinking too much alcohol can cause _____ disease and affect _____ function.

4. Smoking can cause _____ disease, lung disease and lung cancer. It is also linked to mouth, bowel, _____ and _____ cancer.

5. Exposure to _____ (e.g. ionising radiation) can cause _____.

_____ or _____ while pregnant can cause health problems for the unborn baby.

Many non-communicable diseases are caused by several risk factors _____.

Cancer

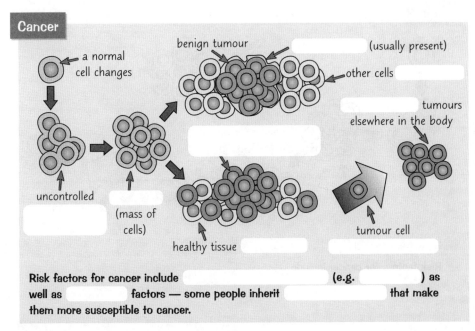

a normal cell changes

benign tumour

_____ (usually present)

other cells _____

_____ tumours elsewhere in the body

uncontrolled _____

_____ (mass of cells)

tumour cell

healthy tissue _____

Risk factors for cancer include _____ (e.g. _____) as well as _____ factors — some people inherit _____ that make them more susceptible to cancer.

Second Go:
..... /..... /.....

Risk Factors for Diseases and Cancer

Five Risk Factors for Non-Communicable Diseases

RISK FACTORS —

(1) _____ are linked to cardiovascular disease.

(2) Obesity is linked to

(3) Drinking too much alcohol can cause

_____ while pregnant
can cause _____
.

(4) Smoking

(5) Exposure to _____ can cause cancer.

Many non-communicable diseases are

Cancer

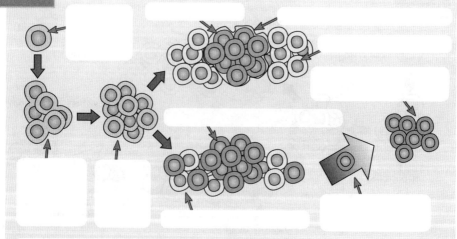

Risk factors for cancer include

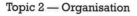

Plant Cell Organisation

Six Plant Tissues

1 Epidermal tissue — covered with a _____ in the leaf to reduce water loss. Cells in the upper layer are transparent to let _____ .

2 Palisade mesophyll tissue — where most _____ happens (so there are lots of _____).

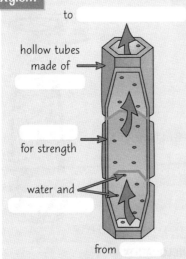

4 Xylem

5 _____

lower epidermal layer

3 _____ tissue — has air spaces to allow the _____ of gases. _____

Leaves are _____ . Together with the roots and stem they form an _____ _____ that _____ substances around the plant.

6 Meristem tissue — found at the _____ . The cells can _____ into many types of cell so the plant can grow.

Xylem

to _____

hollow tubes made of _____

_____ for strength

water and _____

from _____

Xylem tissue carries water in the _____ .

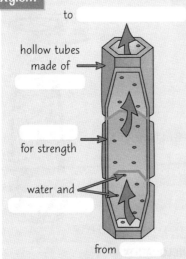

Phloem

elongated _____

small pores in end walls let _____

food substances (mainly _____) are moved from _____ to the rest of the plant

Food molecules can either be _____ or _____ .

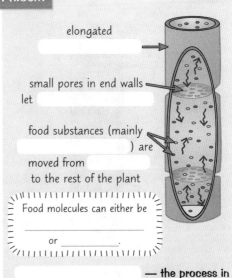

_____ — the process in which food is moved through phloem tubes.

Plant Cell Organisation

Six Plant Tissues

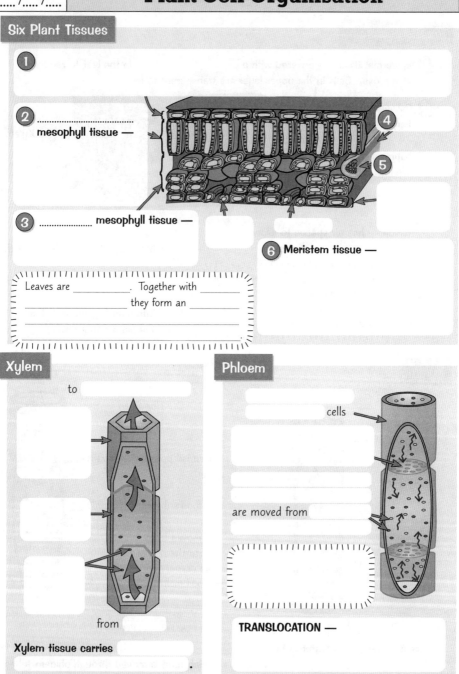

1

2 .... mesophyll tissue —

3 .... mesophyll tissue —

4

5

6 Meristem tissue —

Leaves are _____. Together with _____ they form an _____

Xylem

to _____

from _____

Xylem tissue carries _____

.

Phloem

_____ cells

are moved from _____

TRANSLOCATION —

Transpiration

Transpiration Basics

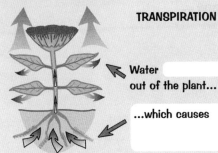

TRANSPIRATION — [_____].

Water [_____] and [_____] out of the plant...

...which causes [_____]

Transpiration Rate

These four things [_____] transpiration rate:

1 Warm temperatures

Water molecules have [_____].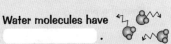

2 [____] light intensity

[_____] when it's light.

3 [____] air flow **4** Low [_____]

[____] water molecules surround the leaves (so there's a [_____] [_____] inside the leaf than outside it).

Guard Cells and Stomata

Guard cells are adapted for [_____] [_____] and controlling [_____].

When the plant has lots of water...

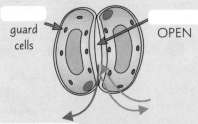

[____] guard cells OPEN

[_____] escapes gases diffuse in and out (e.g. [____] for [_____])

When the plant is short of water or [_____] ...

guard cells

42

Transipration

Transpiration Basics

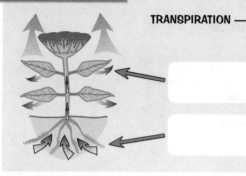

TRANSPIRATION —

Transpiration Rate

These four things increase transpiration rate:

1 temperatures

2 light intensity

3   **4**

Fewer

Guard Cells and Stomata

Guard cells are

When the plant

...

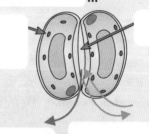

When the plant

or it's dark...

Mixed Practice Quizzes

Well, here we are again. All sorts of stuff was covered over pages 35-42 —
have a go at these quizzes to see how much of it has stuck in your head.

Quiz 1   Date: ...... / ...... / ......

1) What happens to stomata when a plant is in darkness?
2) What is meant by a 'non-communicable' disease?
3) What is phloem tissue made up of?
4) What type of non-communicable disease can be caused by exposure to carcinogens?
5) Describe how water is lost from a plant.
6) How is the structure of spongy mesophyll tissue adapted to its function?
7) True or false? Malignant tumours can form secondary tumours.
8) Other than diseases, name three things that can affect health.
9) What type of cells surround stomata?
10) True or false? Physical illnesses can lead to mental illnesses.

Total:

Quiz 2   Date: ...... / ...... / ......

1) What is the term for a disease that can spread from person to person or between animals and people?
2) List three health problems that are linked to smoking.
3) Which term describes a leaf: a tissue, an organ or an organ system?
4) Under what conditions would a plant's guard cells be flaccid?
5) Give three risk factors for cardiovascular disease.
6) Describe the function of phloem tissue.
7) Which tissue in a leaf is where most photosynthesis happens?
8) Describe two human costs of non-communicable diseases.
9) Describe how a tumour forms.
10) Describe two ways in which epidermal tissue in a leaf is adapted to its function.

Total:

Topic 2 — Organisation

Mixed Practice Quizzes

Quiz 3 Date: ...... / ...... / ......

1) Define 'health'.
2) Give two differences between a benign tumour and a malignant tumour.
3) Describe where meristem tissue is found in a plant.
4) How does the level of humidity affect a plant's transpiration rate?
5) Give two possible health consequences of drinking too much alcohol.
6) Give two examples of allergic reactions that can be triggered by a pathogen infection.
7) What is transpiration?
8) What strengthens the hollow tubes that make up xylem tissue?
9) How can non-communicable diseases have a financial cost on families and the national economy?
10) Describe a risk factor for cancer that is not a lifestyle factor.

Total:

Quiz 4 Date: ...... / ...... / ......

1) What is meant by a 'risk factor' for a non-communicable disease?
2) How are secondary tumours formed?
3) Give one way that a person's life situation might affect their health.
4) What is translocation?
5) How is palisade mesophyll tissue adapted for its function?
6) Name one disease that is linked to obesity.
7) Describe how temperature affects a plant's transpiration rate.
8) What is the function of xylem tissue?
9) What is another health problem that can be triggered by infection by certain viruses?
10) True or false? Guard cells help to control gas exchange in a plant.

Total:

Communicable Disease

First Go:
..... /..... /.....

Infectious Diseases

PATHOGENS — microorganisms that cause ⬚ which ⬚ between organisms.

Disease	Pathogen	How it's spread	Symptoms	Prevention / treatment
Rose black spot	⬚	• Water • ⬚	• ⬚ spots on leaves, can turn yellow and ⬚ • Reduced growth	• Removing and destroying infected leaves • ⬚
Malaria	⬚	⬚ vectors	• ⬚ • Can be ⬚	• ⬚ • Stop mosquitoes from ⬚
⬚ food poisoning	Bacterium	Eating ⬚	• Fever • ⬚ • Vomiting • ⬚	• Vaccination of ⬚ • ⬚ food preparation
Gonorrhoea	⬚	Sexual contact	• Pain when ⬚ • ⬚ discharge from vagina or penis	• Antibiotics
⬚	Virus	⬚ (coughs and sneezes)	• ⬚ • ⬚ skin rash • Can be ⬚	Vaccination of ⬚
HIV	⬚	• Sexual contact • ⬚ (e.g. blood)	• Flu-like (initially) • A damaged ⬚ (late stage infection/AIDS)	• ⬚ • Avoid sharing • ⬚
⬚ virus (TMV)	Virus		⬚ on leaves, which reduces ⬚ and growth	

Communicable Disease

Infectious Diseases

PATHOGENS — microorganisms that

Disease	Pathogen	How it's spread	Symptoms	Prevention / treatment
Rose black spot		• •	• •	• Removing and •
Malaria			• •	• •
	Bacterium		• • Stomach cramps • •	• Vaccination of •
Gonorrhoea			• •	• •
	Virus		• • Red skin rash •	
HIV		• •	• •	• • •
	Virus		Mosaic pattern	

Topic 3 — Infection and Response

Fighting Disease

First Go:
..... /..... /.....

Four Non-Specific Defence Systems Against Pathogens

1 Skin — acts as a _____ and secretes _____ substances to kill pathogens.

2 Nose — _____ and _____ trap particles containing _____ .

3 Trachea and bronchi — mucus _____ pathogens, and _____ waft mucus up to the _____ so that it can be _____ .

4 Stomach — _____ _____ kills pathogens.

Three Ways White Blood Cells Attack Pathogens

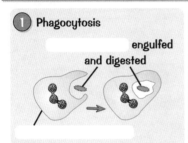

1 Phagocytosis

_____ engulfed and digested

_____

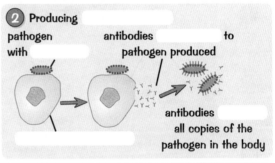

2 Producing _____

pathogen _____ with _____

antibodies _____ to pathogen produced

_____ antibodies _____ all copies of the pathogen in the body

3 Producing _____ — these counteract toxins produced by invading _____ .

Vaccination

Vaccinating a _____ of the population greatly _____ the spread of pathogens so that even people who aren't vaccinated are _____ to catch the disease.

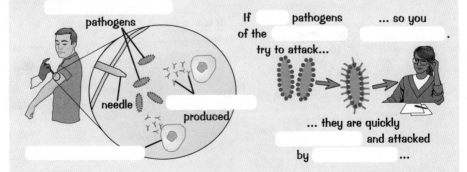

_____

pathogens

needle

_____

_____ produced

If _____ pathogens of the _____ try to attack...

... so you _____ .

... they are quickly _____ and attacked by _____ ...

48

Second Go: ...../...../.....	**Fighting Disease**

Four Non-Specific Defence Systems Against Pathogens

1 Skin —

2 Nose —

3 Trachea and bronchi —

4 Stomach —

Three Ways White Blood Cells Attack Pathogens

1

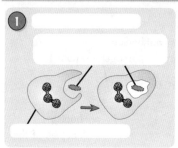

2

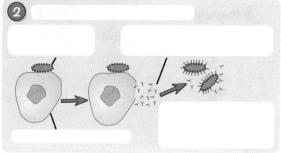

3
Producing _____ — .

Vaccination

Vaccinating a
the spread of pathogens so that

If live

... so

...

... they are

...

Topic 3 — Infection and Response

Mixed Practice Quizzes

Time for more quizzes. Let's see what you've picked up from p.45-48
— knowledge, I mean, not diseases. Mark your answers when you're done.

Quiz 1   Date: ...... / ...... / ......

1) Is measles caused by a bacterium, a fungus or a virus?
2) What type of pathogen causes rose black spot?
3) How is measles spread?
4) True or false? HIV can lead to a damaged immune system.
5) Explain how getting vaccinated against a disease protects you from getting that disease in the future.
6) Give one symptom of malaria.
7) What type of drugs are used to treat HIV?
8) Give four non-specific defence systems present in humans.
9) What happens to the leaves of plants infected by rose black spot?
10) What type of cells produce antibodies and antitoxins?

Total:

Quiz 2   Date: ...... / ...... / ......

1) How are the pathogens given in vaccinations different to those that people might encounter normally?
2) Describe what happens during phagocytosis.
3) How is gonorrhoea spread?
4) Which insect spreads malaria?
5) What part of the body uses hydrochloric acid to kill pathogens?
6) Give two symptoms of measles.
7) How does the skin defend against pathogens?
8) List four symptoms of *Salmonella* food poisoning.
9) What is a pathogen?
10) What is the purpose of antitoxins?

Total:

Mixed Practice Quizzes

Quiz 3 Date: ...... / ...... / ......

1) Give two ways in which the spread of malaria can be prevented.
2) Describe the symptoms of tobacco mosaic virus.
3) How is rose black spot spread?
4) How do people get *Salmonella* food poisoning?
5) The symptoms of HIV are similar to which other disease initially?
6) How can the spread of measles be prevented?
7) What type of pathogen causes HIV?
8) How do the trachea and bronchi defend against pathogens?
9) How can gonorrhoea be treated?
10) True or false? White blood cells produce antigens.

Total:

Quiz 4 Date: ...... / ...... / ......

1) Which of these diseases is caused by a bacterium:
   measles, malaria or gonorrhoea?
2) Give two ways in which HIV is spread.
3) Which condition results from a late stage HIV infection?
4) Give two symptoms of gonorrhoea.
5) Give two ways in which *Salmonella* food poisoning can be prevented.
6) What type of pathogen causes malaria?
7) Give three ways in which white blood cells attack pathogens.
8) How does the nose defend against pathogens?
9) Give two ways in which the spread of rose black spot can be prevented.
10) How does vaccinating a large proportion of a population help to protect
    those who aren't vaccinated from getting a disease?

Total:

Drugs

Types of Drugs

Antibiotics kill [_____].

[_____] antibiotics kill [_____] types of [_____].

Use of [_____] → Deaths from [_____]
Time

It's hard to [_____] that destroy [_____] because they live and reproduce inside [_____].

Painkillers treat the [_____] of disease but don't kill [_____].

Where Drugs Come From

Drug	Type	Source
Digitalis	Heart drug	
	Painkiller	
		Penicillium mould

Nowadays, drugs [_____] in a lab, but the process still might start with a [_____] extracted from a [_____].

[_____] was discovered by Alexander Fleming.

Drug Testing

New drugs are [_____] to check they're [_____].
They are tested for three things:

1 [_____] — how harmful the drug is.

2 Efficacy — whether the drug [_____] and produces the [_____] you're looking for.

3 Dosage — the [_____] that should be given, and [_____] it should be given.

Preclinical Testing

Tests on [_____] and tissues → Tests on [_____] →

Clinical Trials

Tests on [_____]
The dosage is gradually [_____] from a [_____] dose

Clinical trials are often [_____]

Given drug
Given placebo

Tests on [_____]
Finding [_____] dose

PLACEBOS — substances that [_____]
[_____].

52

Drugs

Types of Drugs

Antibiotics _____ .

_____

_____
Time

It's hard to

_____

Painkillers

_____

Where Drugs Come From

Drug	Type	Source

Nowadays,

_____
was discovered by
_____

Drug Testing

New drugs are _____ .
They are tested for three things:

1

2

3

Tests on _____ → Tests on _____ → Tests on _____

Tests on _____

Tests on _____

PLACEBOS —

Monoclonal Antibodies

Monoclonal Antibodies

Monoclonal antibodies are produced from _____ of a _____ _____ (a B-lymphocyte).

Monoclonal antibodies _____ _____ to one protein _____

_____

Produces antibodies

Producing Monoclonal Antibodies

Mouse injected with _____ _____ in lab — don't make antibodies but _____

_____ from mouse — make antibodies but _____

_____ fused with _____

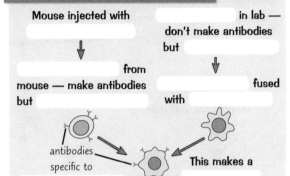

antibodies specific to _____

This makes a _____

It _____ to produce lots of _____ that produce the monoclonal antibodies.

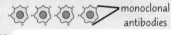

monoclonal antibodies

The antibodies are _____ .

Three Uses of Monoclonal Antibodies

1 Cancer treatment

_____ specific to tumour marker

_____

to stop cells growing and dividing

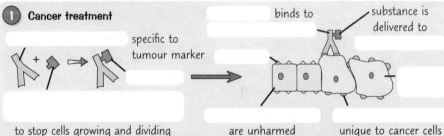

_____ binds to _____

substance is delivered to _____

are unharmed   unique to cancer cells

2 Locating _____ in research

_____ binds to _____ on target molecule and dye is _____

+ : Monoclonal antibodies _____ cells, whereas other _____ may kill any cells.

− : Monoclonal antibody treatments cause more _____ than expected so aren't _____ .

3 Measuring levels of substances _____
E.g. pathogens, hormones and other chemicals.

Pregnancy tests work by _____ in urine.

54

Monoclonal Antibodies

Monoclonal Antibodies

Monoclonal antibodies are

Monoclonal antibodies

Producing Monoclonal Antibodies

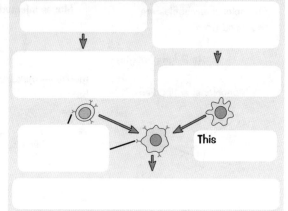

This

The antibodies are

.

Three Uses of Monoclonal Antibodies

① Cancer treatment

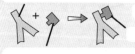

②

in research

+ : Monoclonal antibodies target

− : Monoclonal antibody treatments

③

  ✓ ✓ ✓

Plant Diseases and Defences

Six Signs of Plant Disease

1 _____ growth

2 Spots on _____

3 _____

4 Patches of _____ (rot)

5 Malformed _____

6 _____,
e.g. lumps

Seeing _____
is a sign of an _____.

Causes of Plant Diseases

Plants can be:

Infected by pathogens		
_____	_____	Fungi

_____ by
Insects (e.g. aphids)

Affected by
_____, which stunts growth — _____ are needed to make proteins for growth
_____, which causes chlorosis (yellow leaves) — _____ are needed to make chlorophyll

Three Ways To Identify Plant Disease

1 Look up the signs in a _____ or on a _____.

2 Take the infected plant to a _____, where scientists can identify the _____.

3 Use _____ that identify the pathogen using _____.

Plant Defences

Physical	Mechanical	Chemical
_____ on leaves — barrier to _____.	_____ stop animals touching and eating plants.	kill bacteria and prevent _____.
Layers of _____ around stems (e.g. bark) — barrier to _____.	Leaves that _____ or _____ when touched can knock insects off.	Some plants produce _____ to deter _____.
_____ cell walls — barrier to _____ around cells.	Plants _____ other organisms to trick animals into _____.	

56

Plant Diseases and Defences

Six Signs of Plant Disease

1

2

3

4

5

6

Seeing pests ....
....

Causes of Plant Diseases

Plants can be:

Infected by		

.... by
.... (e.g. aphids)

Affected by
Nitrate deficiency,
Magnesium deficiency,

Three Ways To Identify Plant Disease

1 Look up the signs ....

2 Take the infected plant ....
....

3 Use ....
....

Plant Defences

Physical	Mechanical	Chemical
		Antibacterial chemicals
Layers of		Some plants produce
Cellulose cell walls —		

Mixed Practice Quizzes

That's another topic done and dusted, so try these quizzes based on p.51-56.
Mark each test yourself to see how much you've remembered.

Quiz 1   Date: ...... / ...... / ......

1) Which ion deficiency causes chlorosis in plants?
2) True or false? Painkillers are drugs that can kill pathogens.
3) Why do drugs have to be trialled before they are widely used?
4) Give two examples of chemical defences that plants may have.
5) List three things that new drugs are tested on during preclinical tests.
6) Describe how mice are involved in the production of monoclonal antibodies.
7) What do many plants have around their stems to help protect them from disease?
8) What type of microorganisms do antibiotics kill?
9) Give three uses of monoclonal antibodies.
10) How does mimicking other organisms help to protect a plant?

Total:

Quiz 2   Date: ...... / ...... / ......

1) Give three ways of identifying plant diseases.
2) What type of white blood cell produces monoclonal antibodies?
3) Explain how nitrate deficiency affects plants.
4) What is meant by a 'double-blind' drugs trial?
5) Why is it hard to develop drugs that destroy viruses?
6) What type of drug is digitalis?
7) Give three things that can be attached to monoclonal antibodies used for cancer treatment.
8) Other than pathogens, what else can invade plants and cause disease?
9) Give the three main categories that plant defences can be sorted into.
10) Give one advantage of using monoclonal antibodies as a treatment for cancer.

Total:

Mixed Practice Quizzes

Date: ...... / ...... / ......

1) How are monoclonal antibodies used to locate specific molecules in research?
2) Which antibiotic comes from *Penicillium* mould?
3) Give three mechanical defences used by plants.
4) What organism is the source of aspirin?
5) Why are monoclonal antibody treatments not widely used?
6) What do testing kits use to identify plant diseases?
7) How does the dosage of drugs given change during clinical trials?
8) Why are tumour cells used to produce monoclonal antibodies?
9) What are scientists looking for when testing the toxicity of a new drug?
10) How does a waxy cuticle around its leaves defend a plant from infection?

Total:

Quiz 4   Date: ...... / ...... / ......

1) What is a placebo?
2) How is a hybridoma cell made?
3) How has the increased use of antibiotics affected the number of deaths from bacterial disease?
4) Give six signs of plant disease.
5) Who discovered penicillin?
6) During clinical trials, are drugs tested on: patients, healthy volunteers or both?
7) Give three things that monoclonal antibodies can be used to measure the levels of in blood and urine.
8) Explain how magnesium deficiency affects plants.
9) True or false? One monoclonal antibody can bind to two different types of antigen.
10) What are scientists looking for when testing the efficacy of a new drug?

Total:

Photosynthesis

First Go:
..... /..... /.....

The Photosynthesis Reaction

PHOTOSYNTHESIS — an _____ reaction in which _____ is transferred to chloroplasts from the environment by _____ .

_____ + water ⟶ glucose + _____

6CO₂   6H₂O   60₂

Four Uses of Glucose in Plants

1. _____ — energy is transferred from glucose.

2. Strengthening cell walls — glucose is converted into _____ , which is used to make strong cell walls.

3. Protein synthesis — glucose and _____ are used to make _____ , which are then made into proteins.

4. Energy storage — glucose is turned into _____ or _____ to store energy.

Rate of Photosynthesis

An _____ in any of these four factors tends to increase the _____ of photosynthesis:

1. _____   3. CO₂ concentration

2. _____   4. Amount of chlorophyll

Any of these factors can become the limiting factor (_____
_____).

Rate vs % CO₂ level:
_____ is limiting factor
other factors (e.g. temp or light intensity) _____

temperature is limiting factor
Rate vs Temperature (°C):
high temperatures _____
involved in photosynthesis

Inverse Square Law

The inverse square law links light intensity with _____

_____ :

Light intensity ∝ _____

Greenhouses

You can _____ limiting factors in a greenhouse to _____ , but this _____ .

ventilation   shades
heaters
(_____ for CO₂)

Topic 4 — Bioenergetics

Second Go: ..... / ..... /	**Photosynthesis**

The Photosynthesis Reaction

PHOTOSYNTHESIS — an ⬚⬚⬚⬚⬚⬚ in which ⬚⬚⬚⬚⬚⬚
⬚⬚⬚⬚⬚⬚ by light.

.... + ... ⟶ .... + ...

.... $6H_2O$ ....

Four Uses of Glucose in Plants

1 ⬚⬚⬚⬚⬚⬚ from glucose.

2 ⬚⬚⬚⬚⬚⬚ — glucose is ⬚⬚⬚⬚⬚⬚
⬚⬚⬚⬚⬚⬚, which is used to ⬚⬚⬚⬚⬚⬚ .

3 ⬚⬚⬚⬚⬚⬚ — glucose and ⬚⬚⬚⬚⬚⬚
⬚⬚⬚⬚⬚⬚, which are then made into ⬚⬚⬚⬚⬚⬚ .

4 ⬚⬚⬚⬚⬚⬚ — glucose is turned ⬚⬚⬚⬚⬚⬚
⬚⬚⬚⬚⬚⬚ .

Rate of Photosynthesis

An increase

1   **3**

2   **4** Amount of chlorophyll

Any of these

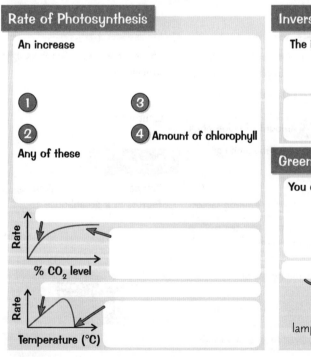

Rate vs % CO_2 level

Rate vs Temperature (°C)

Inverse Square Law

The inverse square law links

Greenhouses

You can control

lamps

Respiration

Energy Transfer

RESPIRATION — the process of transferring energy [   ].
It's an [   ] reaction that goes on continuously in [   ].

The energy transferred is used [   ].
Three examples of these are:

1 To [   ] for movement.

2 To keep warm (in [   ]).

3 To build up [   ] molecules from [   ].

Aerobic Respiration

AEROBIC RESPIRATION —
respiration using [   ]. [   ] + oxygen ⟶ [   ] + water

It's the most [   ]
type of respiration. $C_6H_{12}O_6$ [   ] $6CO_2$ [   ]

Anaerobic Respiration

ANAEROBIC RESPIRATION — respiration [   ].

It transfers [   ] than [   ] respiration
because glucose isn't fully [   ].

In muscle cells:

glucose ⟶ [   ]

In plant and yeast cells:

glucose ⟶ ethanol + [   ]

In yeast cells, anaerobic respiration is called [   ].
The process is used to make [   ].

Respiration

Energy Transfer

RESPIRATION —

It's an

The energy

Three examples of these are:

1

2

3

Aerobic Respiration

AEROBIC RESPIRATION —

It's the

.... + ... ➡ .... + ...

.... $6O_2$ ....

Anaerobic Respiration

ANAEROBIC RESPIRATION —

It transfers

In .... **cells:**   **In plant and** ....

.... ➡ .... ➡ .... + ...

In

The process is used to

Metabolism and Exercise

First Go:
..... / ..... / .....

Metabolism

METABOLISM — the sum of all the _____ that happen
in _____ .

Metabolic reactions use _____
to make new molecules, e.g.:

_____ and nitrate
ions combined to make
amino acids, then
_____ .

Lipids broken down
into _____

_____
joined together to make
bigger _____
(e.g. _____ or glycogen).

Effects of Exercise on the Body

EXERCISE

↓

more .... needed

↓

more ....
.... needed

↓

more .... needed

These three things _____ to
get more _____ to your muscles:

 Heart rate

 _____ rate

 _____

.... also cause muscle fatigue
— the muscles get tired and ....
....

Oxygen Debt

OXYGEN DEBT — _____
_____ oxygen needed to react with
_____ and
remove it from cells.

During _____ ,
not enough oxygen is supplied to
the muscles so:

_____ takes place in muscles

Lactic acid

_____ created

_____ and breathing
rate stay high after exercise
to repay oxygen debt

The _____ also helps deal with lactic acid:

 blood → → blood with
lactic acid →

lactic acid converted to _____

Topic 4 — Bioenergetics

Metabolism and Exercise

Metabolism

METABOLISM —

Metabolic reactions use

Effects of Exercise on the Body

EXERCISE

These three things increase to

Long

 — the muscles get

Oxygen Debt

OXYGEN DEBT —

During vigorous exercise,

Anaerobic respiration

repay oxygen debt

The liver

:

blood → muscle → blood with → liver

  ✓ ✓ ✓

Mixed Practice Quizzes

All that talk of exercise is enough to make me feel out of breath, but we've made it to the end of the topic already — phew. Time to test yourself on p.59-64.

Quiz 1   Date: ...... / ...... / ......

1) True or false? Photosynthesis is an endothermic reaction.
2) What is respiration?
3) List four factors that tend to increase the rate of photosynthesis.
4) Which type of respiration is more efficient, aerobic or anaerobic?
5) Give two things that plants convert glucose to for storage.
6) Which type of respiration doesn't use oxygen?
7) Which two factors are linked by the inverse square law?
8) What are the products of anaerobic respiration in yeast cells?
9) In plants, what is needed in addition to glucose to make proteins?
10) Explain how exercise affects the body's need for oxygen.

Total:

Quiz 2   Date: ...... / ...... / ......

1) Give the word equation for aerobic respiration.
2) Give three processes that energy transferred by respiration is used for.
3) What effect does a decrease in the CO_2 concentration tend to have on the rate of photosynthesis?
4) What is anaerobic respiration in yeast cells called?
5) What does it mean if something is a limiting factor of photosynthesis?
6) List three things that increase to supply more oxygen to the muscles during exercise.
7) What is the formula for the inverse square law?
8) How does the liver help to deal with built-up lactic acid?
9) Give the word equation for anaerobic respiration in plant cells.
10) What effect does fatigue have on muscle contraction?

Total:

Topic 4 — Bioenergetics

Mixed Practice Quizzes

Quiz 3

Date: ...... / ...... / ......

1) During photosynthesis, energy is transferred from the environment to which subcellular structure?

2) Is respiration an endothermic or exothermic reaction?

3) Which process transfers energy from glucose?

4) Give the word equation for photosynthesis.

5) What effect does an increase in light intensity tend to have on the rate of photosynthesis?

6) What are the products of aerobic respiration?

7) Explain why an oxygen debt is created during vigorous exercise.

8) True or false? Anaerobic respiration in muscle cells produces lactic acid.

9) Give four uses of glucose in plants.

10) What molecule is represented by the chemical formula $C_6H_{12}O_6$?

Total:

Quiz 4

Date: ...... / ...... / ......

1) Give one disadvantage of controlling limiting factors in a greenhouse.

2) Why does anaerobic respiration transfer less energy than aerobic respiration?

3) Give an example of a food product that fermentation is used to make.

4) Define 'metabolism'.

5) Why does breath volume increase during exercise?

6) Why does photosynthesis stop at high temperatures?

7) What process is represented by this equation:
$6CO_2 + 6H_2O \rightarrow C_6H_{12}O_6 + 6O_2$?

8) What is meant by oxygen debt?

9) How do plants use glucose to strengthen their cell walls?

10) Give one example of how energy from respiration is used to make new molecules.

Total:

Topic 4 — Bioenergetics

Homeostasis and the Nervous System

Maintaining a Stable Internal Environment

HOMEOSTASIS — the _____ inside your _____. It maintains a stable internal environment in response to changes in _____ conditions.

Homeostasis maintains optimal conditions for _____.

Component of control systems	Function of component
Receptors	To detect _____ (changes in _____)
	To _____ and _____ information from receptors and organise a _____
Effectors	To produce a response to _____ and restore _____

Automatic control systems can involve _____ or _____ responses.

Three things in your body that are _____ by control systems:

 1 _____   2 _____   3 _____

The Nervous System

NEURONES — cells that _____ as _____ in the nervous system. The nervous system means that humans can _____ and _____.

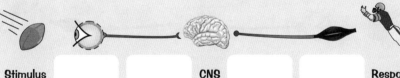

Stimulus   CNS   Response

CENTRAL NERVOUS SYSTEM (CNS) — consists of the _____ and _____. It is connected to the body by _____ neurones and _____ neurones.

Effectors can be _____ (which respond to nervous impulses by contracting) or _____ (which secrete hormones).

 ☑   ☑   ☑

Homeostasis and the Nervous System

Maintaining a Stable Internal Environment

HOMEOSTASIS —

Homeostasis maintains

Component of control systems	Function of component
Receptors	
	To from receptors
Effectors	

[   ] can involve [   ] or [   ] responses.

Three things in your body that are [   ]:

1 [   ] **2** [   ] **3** [   ]

The Nervous System

NEURONES — cells that [   ]
[   ]. **The nervous system means that humans can**
[   ].

CENTRAL NERVOUS SYSTEM (CNS) —

It is

Effectors can be _____ (which
_____) or
(which _____).

Synapses, Reflexes and the Brain

Synapses

SYNAPSE — the [_____]
between two [_____].
A nerve signal is transferred
across a [_____] by the
[_____].

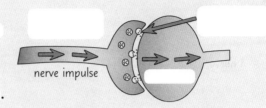

nerve impulse

Reflex Arcs

REFLEXES — [_____], [_____] responses to certain [_____] that don't involve
the [_____]. They can reduce the chance of [_____].

Five steps in a reflex arc:

①	Stimulation of ....
②	Impulses travel along ....
③	Impulses passed along ....
④	Impulses travel along ....
⑤	.... contracts and arm moves

The Brain

BRAIN — the organ in charge of [_____].
It is made up of billions of [_____].

Three methods for
[_____] the brain:

① Observe patients with
[_____]

② [_____]
parts of the brain

③ Use [_____] scanners

e.g. consciousness,
intelligence,
memory, language

Front   Back

muscle
coordination

unconscious activities

The brain is .... and ....,
so investigating or treating it is .... and ....

Synapses, Reflexes and the Brain

Synapses

SYNAPSE —

A nerve signal

Reflex Arcs

REFLEXES — _____ that don't involve
the _____ . They can _____ .

Five steps in a _____ :

1	
2	
3	
4	
5	

The Brain

BRAIN — _____ .
It is _____ .

Three methods for
studying the brain:

Front   Back

1

2

3

The brain is _____
_____ .

Topic 5 — Homeostasis and Response

The Eye

Structure of the Eye

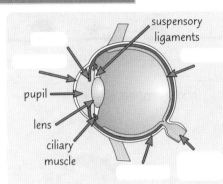

suspensory ligaments

pupil

lens

ciliary muscle

Sclera	,	wall
Cornea	outer layer at	
Iris	Contains controlling	
Retina	Contains cells sensitive to	
Optic nerve	from receptor cells to	

Eye Reflexes

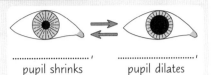

.... , ... ,
pupil shrinks   pupil dilates

ACCOMMODATION — the lens
to focus light on the .

ciliary muscles   lens becomes

near object

light refracted

suspensory ligaments

ciliary muscles   lens becomes

distant object

suspensory ligaments

light refracted

Common Defects of the Eye

Long-sightedness (**):**   **Short-sightedness (** **):**

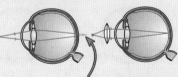   

Image of brought into focus retina.

Fixed using lens.

Image of brought into focus in front of retina.

Fixed using lens.

These defects are usually treated by **— three other options are:**

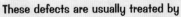

1   **2** surgery   **3** surgery

The Eye

Structure of the Eye

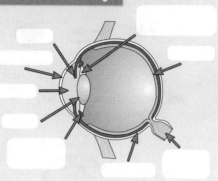

Sclera	
Cornea	
Iris	
Retina	
Optic nerve	

Eye Reflexes

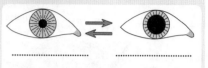

....
....

ACCOMMODATION — the lens

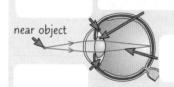

near object

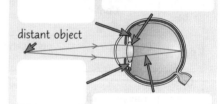

distant object

Common Defects of the Eye

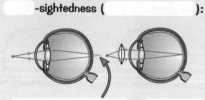

-sightedness ( ):

Fixed using

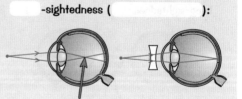

-sightedness ( ):

Fixed using

These defects are usually _____ — three other options are:

1 _____   2 _____   3 _____

Topic 5 — Homeostasis and Response

  ✓ ✓ ✓

Mixed Practice Quizzes

It's time to get your eyes in focus and really ramp-up your brain activity by
having a go at these quizzes. The questions are all based on p.67-72. Good luck.

Quiz 1   Date: ...... / ...... / ......

1) What is a neurone?
2) What happens to your pupils when you move from an area with
   bright light to one with dim light?
3) Do reflexes involve the conscious or unconscious parts of the brain?
4) Define 'homeostasis'.
5) What two things are receptor cells in the eye sensitive to?
6) Why do humans need a nervous system?
7) What would someone with myopia have difficulty seeing —
   an object that's close up or one that's far away?
8) How is a nerve signal transferred across a synapse?
9) What are the three components of a control system in the body?
10) What is the brain made up of?

Total:

Quiz 2   Date: ...... / ...... / ......

1) What is the role of the sclera in the eye?
2) What are stimuli?
3) What is the role of a coordination centre in a control system?
4) What other term is used for long-sightedness?
5) What is the role of the brain?
6) What type of neurone passes impulses from a sensory neurone
   to a motor neurone in a reflex arc?
7) What is a synapse?
8) How is homeostasis important for enzyme action?
9) Which part of the brain controls unconscious activities?
10) How are eye defects usually treated?

Total:

Mixed Practice Quizzes

Quiz 3   Date: ...... / ...... / ......

1) Why are reflex arcs important?
2) What does the cerebellum control?
3) How do concave lenses treat myopia?
4) What happens in the process of accommodation?
5) Why is the brain difficult to study and treat?
6) Which two structures does the central nervous system consist of?
7) Give the name of the transparent outer layer at the front of the eye.
8) What is the role of an effector in a control system?
9) How do ciliary muscles change to allow distant objects to be seen in focus?
10) Which type of neurone passes impulses from the CNS to effectors?

Total:

Quiz 4   Date: ...... / ...... / ......

1) Give three methods of studying the brain.
2) Which structure associated with the eye carries impulses from receptor cells to the brain?
3) What happens to the shape of the lens when the suspensory ligaments relax?
4) What type of neurone connects receptors to the central nervous system?
5) How is the structure of the iris related to its function?
6) Give three functions of the cerebral cortex.
7) Give three examples of things in the body that are maintained by automatic control systems.
8) Give three options for treating eye defects other than wearing glasses.
9) In people with hyperopia, where is the image of an object brought into focus in relation to the retina?
10) Give two different types of effector in the body.

Total:

Topic 5 — Homeostasis and Response

Body Temperature and Hormones

Controlling Body Temperature

There are temperature receptors in the [   ] and
the [   ] of the brain.

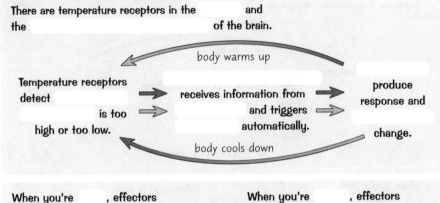

body warms up

Temperature receptors
detect [   ]
[   ] is too
high or too low.

receives information from [   ]
and triggers [   ]
automatically.

produce
response and [   ]
change.

body cools down

When you're [   ], effectors
help to transfer energy from the
[   ] to the [   ]:

When you're [   ], effectors
reduce the energy transferred
to the [   ]:

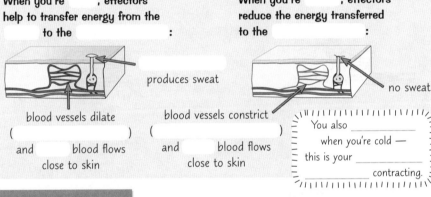

produces sweat

no sweat

blood vessels dilate
([   ])
and [   ] blood flows
close to skin

blood vessels constrict
([   ])
and [   ] blood flows
close to skin

You also [   ]
when you're cold —
this is your [   ]
[   ] contracting.

The Endocrine System

ENDOCRINE SYSTEM — made up
of [   ] that secrete chemicals
(known as [   ]) directly into
the [   ], which carries
them to the [   ].

'master gland',
stimulates other glands

produces thyroxine

[   ] (male)
produce testosterone

produces adrenaline

produces insulin

The effects of hormones
are [   ] than nerves
but last [   ].

[   ] (female)
produce oestrogen

Topic 5 — Homeostasis and Response

Body Temperature and Hormones

Controlling Body Temperature

There are temperature receptors

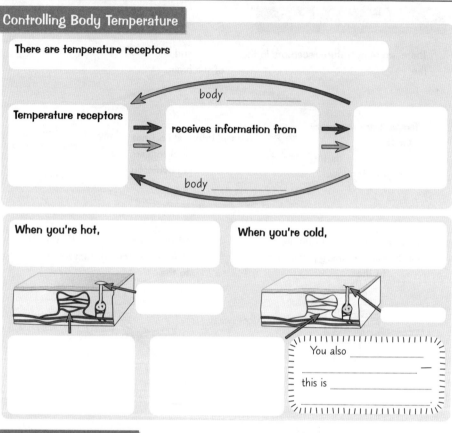

Temperature receptors → receives information from →

body _____

body _____

When you're hot,

When you're cold,

You also _____ —

this is _____

The Endocrine System

ENDOCRINE SYSTEM —

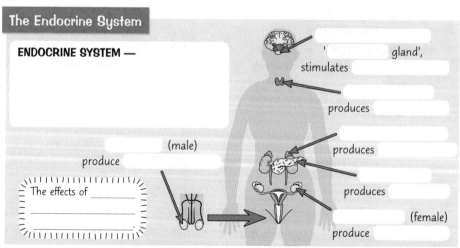

' _____ gland',
stimulates _____

produces _____

produces _____

produces _____

(male)
produce _____

The effects of _____

(female)
produce _____

Blood Glucose and Hormones

Controlling Blood Glucose

Five steps to reduce blood glucose:

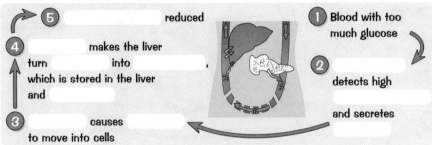

5 _____ reduced

4 _____ makes the liver turn _____ into _____, which is stored in the liver and _____

3 _____ causes _____ to move into cells

1 Blood with too much glucose

2 _____ detects high _____ and secretes _____

Five steps to increase blood glucose:

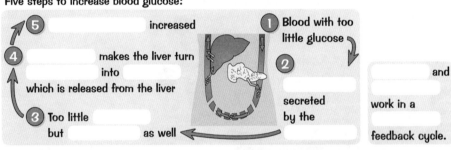

5 _____ increased

4 _____ makes the liver turn _____ into _____ which is released from the liver

3 Too little _____ but _____ as well

1 Blood with too little glucose

2 _____ secreted by the _____

_____ and _____ work in a _____ feedback cycle.

Diabetes

	Type 1	Type 2
Cause	Pancreas produces _____ insulin	_____ no longer respond to _____ properly
Effect	_____ rise to _____ levels	
Treatment	Insulin _____	_____ controlled diet and regular _____

_____ is a major risk factor for _____ diabetes.

Adrenaline and Thyroxine

Adrenaline released in response to _____ → Increases _____

Increases supply of _____ to muscles and brain → Readies body for '_____'

Thyroxine plays a role in regulating the _____ and is important for _____ synthesis for _____.

_____ levels are controlled by negative feedback.

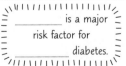

Topic 5 — Homeostasis and Response

Blood Glucose and Hormones

Controlling Blood Glucose

Five steps to reduce blood glucose:

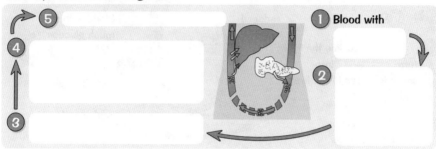

1. Blood with
2.
3.
4.
5.

Five steps to increase blood glucose:

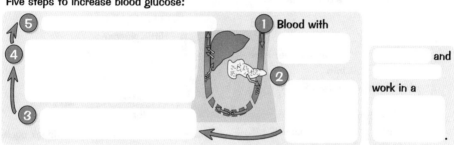

1. Blood with
2.
3.
4.
5.

and

work in a

.

Diabetes

	Type 1	Type 2
Cause		
Effect		
Treatment		and

Adrenaline and Thyroxine

Adrenaline released

Increases supply of

Thyroxine plays a role in

and

is important for

.

are controlled

by .

Topic 5 — Homeostasis and Response

Waste Substances and the Kidneys

Waste Substances

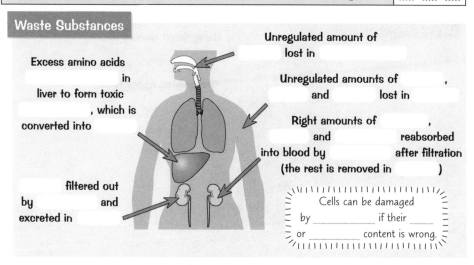

Excess amino acids _____ in liver to form toxic _____, which is converted into _____

_____ filtered out by _____ and excreted in _____

Unregulated amount of _____ lost in _____

Unregulated amounts of _____, _____ and _____ lost in _____

Right amounts of _____, _____ and _____ reabsorbed into blood by _____ after filtration (the rest is removed in _____)

Cells can be damaged by _____ if their _____ or _____ content is wrong.

Controlling the Concentration of Urine

The concentration of urine is controlled by _____ hormone (ADH).

Brain detects _____ is too high ⇒ _____ releases less _____ ⇒ Less _____ is reabsorbed from _____

water content

water content

Brain detects _____ is too low → _____ releases more _____ → More _____ is reabsorbed from _____

Kidney Failure

People with kidney failure need to have _____.

Healthy kidneys can be _____ from _____.

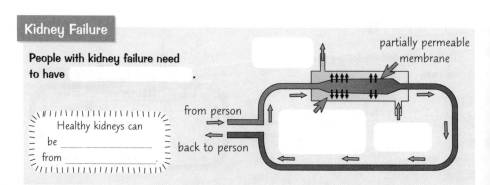

partially permeable membrane

from person

back to person

Waste Substances and the Kidneys

Waste Substances

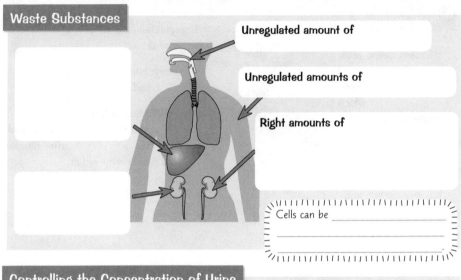

Unregulated amount of

Unregulated amounts of

Right amounts of

Cells can be _____
_____
_____

Controlling the Concentration of Urine

The concentration of urine is controlled by _____ .

Brain detects ⟹ releases ⟹

water content decreases

water content increases

Brain detects ⟹ releases ⟹

Kidney Failure

People with kidney failure need to have _____ .

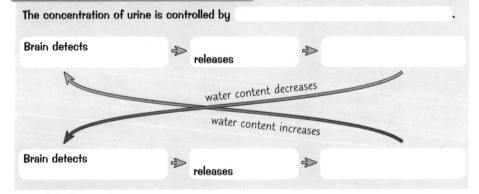

_____ can
be _____
from _____ .

Mixed Practice Quizzes

You've got to be kidneying me (I know), it's time for some more practice quizzes.
These questions are based on p.75-80. Don't forget to tick the ones you get right.

Quiz 1   Date: ...... / ...... / ......

1) What hormone is produced in the testes?
2) Briefly describe what happens when a person's blood passes through a dialysis machine.
3) List three ways that your body responds when you're too cold.
4) What substance is ammonia converted to in the liver?
5) Describe the cause of Type 2 diabetes.
6) How does adrenaline help to increase the supply of oxygen and glucose to the muscles and the brain?
7) Other than the brain, where in the body are temperature receptors found?
8) Which gland is known as the 'master gland'?
9) Name three substances that are lost in sweat.
10) Give two responses to insulin that reduce blood glucose level.

Total:

Quiz 2   Date: ...... / ...... / ......

1) What is the endocrine system?
2) Why is it important that the water and ion content of cells is controlled?
3) What happens to excess amino acids in the body?
4) How and why does the blood's water content change if more ADH is released into the blood?
5) True or false? In Type 1 diabetes, the pancreas produces too much insulin.
6) Which hormone helps to regulate the basal metabolic rate?
7) Which hormone is released when blood glucose level is too high?
8) Which organs are responsible for filtering out urea?
9) How does vasodilation help to cool the body?
10) Is obesity a major risk factor for Type 1 diabetes or Type 2 diabetes?

Total:

Mixed Practice Quizzes

Quiz 3 Date: ...... / ...... / ......

1) Which organ detects changes in blood glucose level? ☑
2) True or false? The body regulates the amount of water that's lost in exhalation. ☑
3) How do hormones travel around the body to reach target organs? ☑
4) Give two possible treatments for people with kidney failure. ☑
5) a) Which two hormones control blood glucose level?
   b) Which of these hormones acts to increase blood glucose level? ☑
6) What is the role of the thermoregulatory centre in the brain? ☑
7) Which hormone is released in response to fear or stress? ☑
8) Give two ways in which the body responds when core body temperature is too high. ☑
9) Which hormone controls the water content of the blood? ☑
10) Which gland produces thyroxine? ☑

Total: ☐

Quiz 4 Date: ...... / ...... / ......

1) In which organ are excess amino acids deaminated? ☑
2) What hormone is produced by the ovaries? ☑
3) True or false? Thyroxine level is controlled by negative feedback. ☑
4) Give two ways in which the effects of hormones and nerves are different. ☑
5) What is the treatment for: a) Type 1 diabetes?   b) Type 2 diabetes? ☑
6) What hormone is produced by the adrenal glands? ☑
7) Explain how blood glucose level is returned to normal once the body has detected it's too low. ☑
8) Name three substances that are reabsorbed by the kidneys into the blood after filtration. ☑
9) How does the pituitary gland react if the blood's water content is too high? ☑
10) How is excess urea excreted from the body? ☑

Total: ☐

Topic 5 — Homeostasis and Response

Puberty and the Menstrual Cycle

Puberty and Sex Hormones

PUBERTY — when the body starts releasing [ ], which trigger the development of [ ] (e.g. facial hair in men and breasts in women).

In men, the main reproductive hormone is [ ], which stimulates [ ].

In women, the main reproductive hormone is [ ].

The Menstrual Cycle

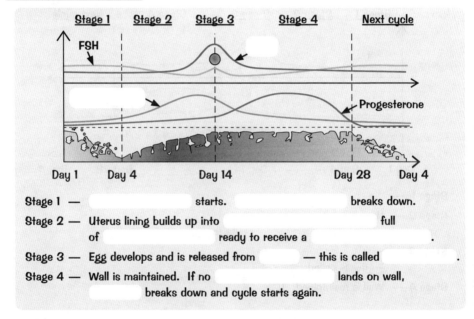

Stage 1   Stage 2   Stage 3   Stage 4   Next cycle

FSH

Progesterone

Day 1   Day 4   Day 14   Day 28   Day 4

Stage 1 — [ ] starts. [ ] breaks down.

Stage 2 — Uterus lining builds up into [ ] full of [ ] ready to receive a [ ].

Stage 3 — Egg develops and is released from [ ] — this is called [ ].

Stage 4 — Wall is maintained. If no [ ] lands on wall, [ ] breaks down and cycle starts again.

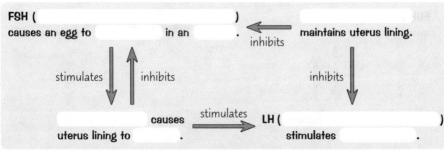

FSH ([ ] **)**
causes an egg to [ ] in an [ ].

[ ] maintains uterus lining.

inhibits

stimulates   *inhibits*   *inhibits*

[ ] uterus lining to [ ].

causes   *stimulates*   **LH (** [ ] **)** stimulates [ ].

Puberty and the Menstrual Cycle

Puberty and Sex Hormones

PUBERTY — when the _____ ,
which _____
_____ (e.g. facial hair in men and breasts in women).

In men,

In women,

The Menstrual Cycle

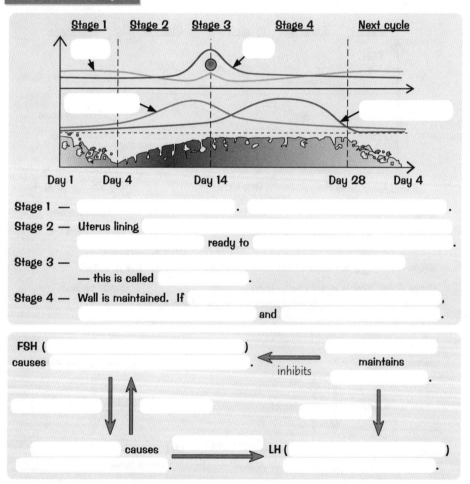

Stage 1   Stage 2   Stage 3   Stage 4   Next cycle

Day 1   Day 4   Day 14   Day 28   Day 4

Stage 1 — _____ . _____ .

Stage 2 — Uterus lining _____
_____ ready to _____ .

Stage 3 — _____
_____ — this is called _____ .

Stage 4 — Wall is maintained. If _____ ,
_____ and _____ .

FSH (_____)
causes _____ .   *inhibits*   maintains _____ .

_____   _____   _____

_____ causes _____ → LH (_____)
_____ .   _____ .

Topic 5 — Homeostasis and Response

Controlling Fertility

Reducing Fertility

CONTRACEPTION — methods of _____ the likelihood of _____ reaching an ovulated egg.

Hormonal methods	Non-hormonal methods
Oral contraceptive pills contain _____ that inhibit ____ and stop _____	_____ and _____ physically prevent sperm from reaching egg.
The contraceptive implant releases _____ continuously to stop _____ and _____ of eggs.	Sterilisation — a _____ surgical procedure to stop a man or woman from _____.
Injections or _____ work in a similar way to implants but _____.	_____ disable or kill sperm.
_____ are inserted into uterus to prevent _____ (may also release _____).	_____ from sexual intercourse completely.

Increasing Fertility

Women who _____ can be given a fertility drug containing _____.
If a woman can't get pregnant using _____, she may choose to try ____ :

The woman is given _____ to stimulate _____ to mature.

⬇

The eggs are collected from the _____.

⬇

The eggs are fertilised in a lab using the _____.

IVF stands for
"
_____ "

⬇

The _____ are grown into _____.

⬇

Once the _____ are _____, one or two
of them are transferred to the _____.

Three _____ of IVF:

1 It's emotionally and physically _____. 2 _____ success rate.

3 Can lead to _____, which can be _____ for mother and babies.

Controlling Fertility

Reducing Fertility

CONTRACEPTION —

Hormonal methods	Non-hormonal methods
Oral contraceptive pills	Condoms and
The contraceptive implant	Sterilisation —
Injections or	

Increasing Fertility

Women who _____ can be given _____ .

If a woman _____ , she may choose to try _____ :

The woman is given _____ .

⬇

The eggs are _____ .

⬇

The eggs are _____ .

⬇

The _____ are

_____ .

_____ stands for
"_____"

⬇

Once the _____ , one or two

of them are _____ .

Three _____ of IVF:

1 _____ 2 _____

3 _____

Plant Hormones

Phototropism

AUXIN — a plant hormone that [_____] near the tips of [_____] and [_____].

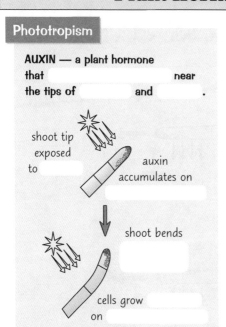

shoot tip exposed to [_____]

auxin accumulates on [_____]

shoot bends

cells grow on [_____]

Gravitropism/Geotropism

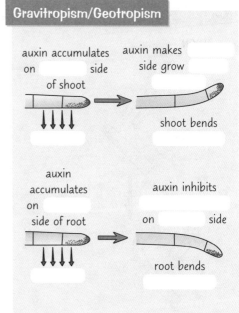

auxin accumulates on [____] side of shoot

auxin makes [____] side grow

shoot bends

auxin accumulates on [____] side of root

auxin inhibits [____] on [____] side

root bends

Commercial Uses of Plant Hormones

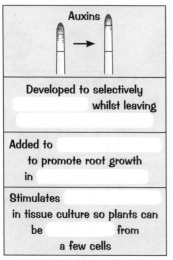

Auxins

Developed to selectively [_____] whilst leaving [_____]

Added to [_____] to promote root growth in [_____]

Stimulates [_____] in tissue culture so plants can be [_____] from a few cells

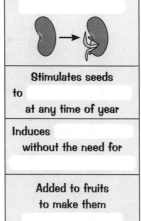

[_____]

Stimulates seeds to [_____] at any time of year

Induces [_____] without the need for [_____]

Added to fruits to make them [_____]

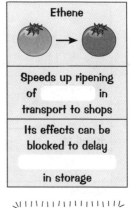

Ethene

Speeds up ripening of [_____] in transport to shops

Its effects can be blocked to delay [_____] in storage

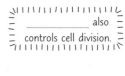

[_____] also controls cell division.

Topic 5 — Homeostasis and Response

Plant Hormones

Phototropism

AUXIN —

exposed
to

Gravitropism/Geotropism

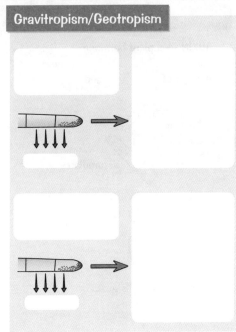

Commercial Uses of Plant Hormones

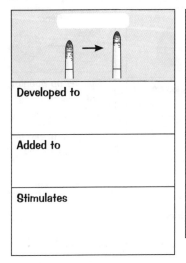

Developed to

Added to

Stimulates

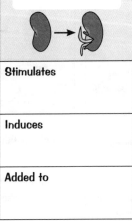

Stimulates

Induces

Added to

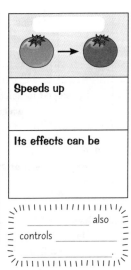

Speeds up

Its effects can be

_____ also
controls _____
_____.

Topic 5 — Homeostasis and Response

Mixed Practice Quizzes

Nice one, you've made it to the end of the topic. Hopefully you'll know enough from p.83-88 to be able to ace these four fabulous practice quizzes.

Quiz 1   Date: ...... / ...... / ......

1) Which plant hormone is added to rooting powders?
2) How do oral contraceptive pills work?
3) Which two hormones are given to women in fertility drugs?
4) Approximately how often does ovulation occur?
5) Which hormone stimulates sperm production in men?
6) How do diaphragms prevent pregnancy?
7) What is the role of FSH in the menstrual cycle?
8) Where does auxin accumulate in a shoot exposed to light?
9) What is ovulation?
10) Give three commercial uses of gibberellin.

Total:

Quiz 2   Date: ...... / ...... / ......

1) What is gravitropism?
2) During IVF, where are embryos transferred to once they are tiny balls of cells?
3) Which two hormones does progesterone inhibit?
4) Give three commercial uses of auxins.
5) What is the main reproductive hormone in women?
6) What is the purpose of contraception?
7) Which hormone stimulates ovulation?
8) Which plant hormone can be added to fruits to make them grow larger?
9) How do intrauterine devices prevent pregnancy?
10) Which plant hormone speeds up the ripening of fruit?

Total:

Topic 5 — Homeostasis and Response

Mixed Practice Quizzes

Quiz 3
Date: ...... / ...... / ......

1) Which hormone causes an egg to mature in an ovary?
2) Which plant hormone has been developed into selective weedkillers?
3) How does accumulated auxin on the lower side of a root cause it to bend downwards?
4) Give three negative aspects of IVF.
5) Which contraceptive method disables or kills sperm?
6) How are eggs fertilised in IVF?
7) Give two examples of hormonal contraceptive methods.
8) What triggers the development of secondary sexual characteristics during puberty?
9) True or false? Auxin inhibits growth in shoot tips.
10) Which two hormones are responsible for the growth and maintenance of the uterus lining?

Total:

Quiz 4
Date: ...... / ...... / ......

1) Which hormone does oestrogen: a) stimulate?   b) inhibit?
2) What is phototropism?
3) What is the purpose of IVF?
4) What word is used to describe the growth of plants in response to light?
5) Why are FSH and LH given to a woman who is undergoing IVF?
6) Give two examples of non-hormonal contraceptive methods.
7) Which plant hormone can be used to delay the ripening of fruits in storage?
8) How often is an egg released from an ovary once a female has reached puberty?
9) Give three hormonal contraceptive methods that work by releasing progesterone.
10) What is sterilisation (in terms of contraception)?

Total:

DNA

Genetic Material

DeoxyriboNucleic Acid — the chemical a cell's _____ is made from.

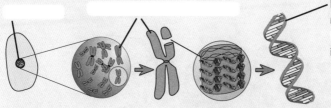

DNA is a
made up of
_____ coiled
into a
_____ .

CHROMOSOMES — _____ of DNA that normally come in _____ .

Humans have _____ pairs. The 23rd pair carries genes which decide a person's _____ .

| XY | |
| XX | |

Genes

GENE — a _____ of
DNA found on a _____ .

Each gene codes for a particular
sequence of _____ ,
which are put together to make a
_____ .

20 different _____

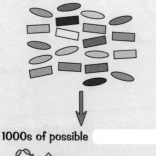

1000s of possible _____

Genomes

GENOME — an organism's entire
set of _____ .

The complete _____

has been worked out.

_____ linked
to diseases can be
_____ .

Tiny differences in
_____

can be studied.

This helps us
better understand

_____

so we can develop
effective treatments.

This helps us trace
the migration
patterns of

_____ .

DNA

Genetic Material

D_____N_____A_____ —

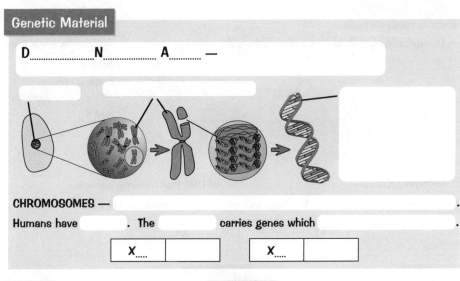

CHROMOSOMES —

Humans have [   ]. The [   ] carries genes which [   ].

X.....	

X.....	

Genes

GENE —

Each gene codes for

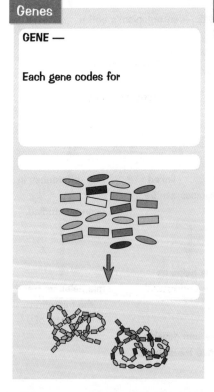

Genomes

GENOME —

The complete

Genes linked to

can be studied.

This helps us better

This helps us trace

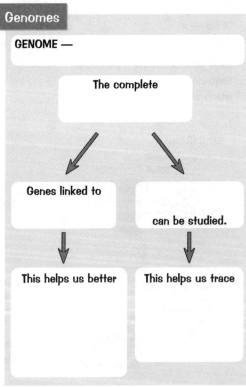

DNA, Proteins and Mutations

The Structure of DNA

Part of a DNA strand

backbone

one of the

Complementary base pairs

A

G

Part of a
DNA molecule

base on

is joined to a
on the
other strand

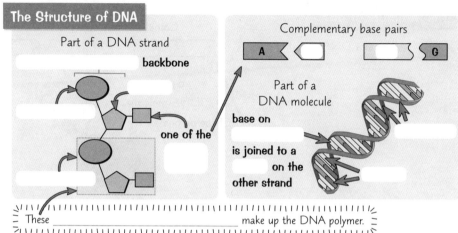

These .... make up the DNA polymer.

Protein Synthesis

Each .... is coded for
by a sequence of ....

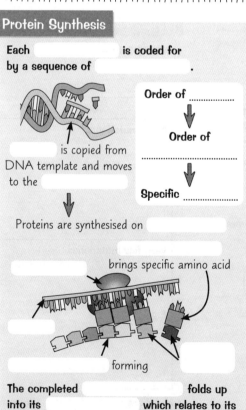

.... is copied from
DNA template and moves
to the ....

Order of ....

↓

Order of
....

↓

Specific ....

Proteins are synthesised on ....

.... brings specific amino acid

.... forming ....

The completed .... folds up
into its .... which relates to its
function — e.g. a structural protein like collagen.

Mutations

MUTATIONS — .... to
the sequence of ....
They occur ....

	Effect
Most mutations	.... on the protein.
Some mutations	Alter the protein .... but its .... are not affected.
Very few mutations	Change the shape of the .... and affect its .... E.g. an enzyme substrate no longer fits or a structural protein ....

Mutations in non-coding DNA can
alter ....

DNA, Proteins and Mutations

The Structure of DNA

Part of a DNA strand

Complementary base pairs

Part of a
DNA molecule

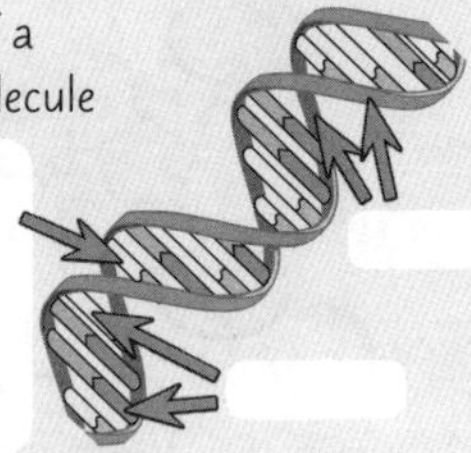

base on one

These _____ make up the _____.

Protein Synthesis

Each amino acid

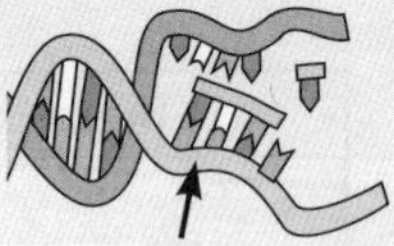

_____ is copied from
_____ and moves

to the _____

Proteins are synthesised on ribosomes.

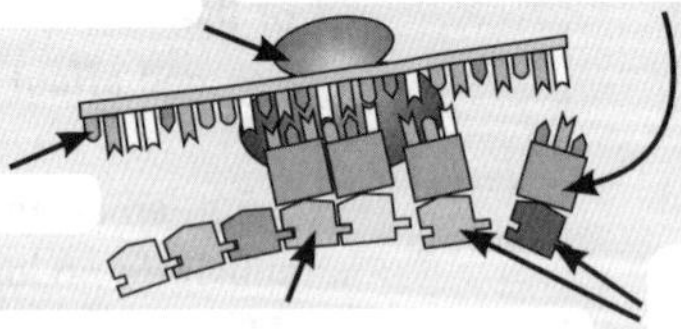

The completed protein

Mutations

MUTATIONS —

Effect
Most mutations:
Some mutations:
Very few mutations:
E.g.

Mutations in _____ DNA can
alter _____.

Reproduction

Asexual and Sexual Reproduction

	Asexual	Sexual
Parents		
Cell division		Meiosis and mitosis
Produces	[____] offspring	Offspring containing a [____] of the parents' genes
Advantages	[____] compared to sexual reproduction, so many identical offspring can be produced in [ ] Only [____] needed so no energy is wasted finding a mate.	The [____] produced in the offspring increases the chance that some individuals of a species will survive a [____]. We can use [____] to utilise the variation in offspring and increase [____].

Some organisms can [____] depending on the circumstances.
E.g. the [____] parasite reproduces sexually in mosquitoes and asexually in humans.

Meiosis

Meiosis produces cells with [____].

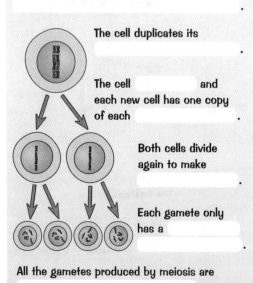

The cell duplicates its [____].

The cell [____] and each new cell has one copy of each [____].

Both cells divide again to make [____].

Each gamete only has a [____].

All the gametes produced by meiosis are [____].

Gametes

Gametes are formed by [____] in the [____].

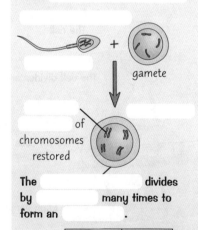

[____] + [____] gamete

[____] of chromosomes restored

The [____] divides by [____] many times to form an [____].

	Animal	Plant
M		Pollen
F	Egg	

Reproduction

Asexual and Sexual Reproduction

	Asexual	Sexual
Parents		
Cell division		
Produces		
Advantages	Fast compared to Only one parent	The variation produced in the offspring We can use

Some organisms can

. E.g.

.

Meiosis

Meiosis produces cells

The cell

The cell divides and

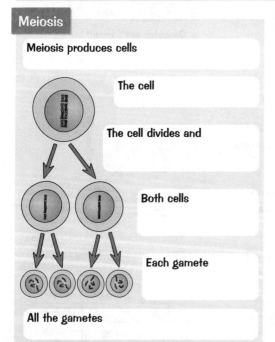

Both cells

Each gamete

All the gametes

Gametes

Gametes are formed

gamete +

gamete

offspring

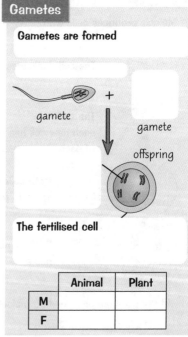

The fertilised cell

	Animal	Plant
M		
F		

Mixed Practice Quizzes

Congrats, you've reached the next set of quizzes. This lot of questions are based on p.91-96 so prepare to spill all you know about DNA, proteins and reproduction.

Quiz 1   Date: ...... / ...... / ......

1) Give the names of the gametes produced by plants.
2) True or false? Bases are attached to phosphates in DNA molecules.
3) Which is faster: asexual reproduction or sexual reproduction?
4) How many pairs of chromosomes do human body cells have?
5) How many parents are needed for asexual reproduction?
6) What are the repeating units of DNA called?
7) True or false? Mutations occur continuously.
8) How many gametes are produced from a single cell undergoing meiosis?
9) What is the complementary DNA base to A?
10) How does the order of bases in a gene determine the protein that is made?

Total:

Quiz 2   Date: ...... / ...... / ......

1) Give two advantages of asexual reproduction over sexual reproduction.
2) What is a gene?
3) Which type of reproduction involves meiosis: asexual or sexual?
4) True or false? Most mutations alter the functions of proteins.
5) How can variation in offspring from sexual reproduction be advantageous?
6) How many strands is a DNA molecule made up of?
7) How many pairs of a person's chromosomes determine their sex?
8) Describe the role of carrier molecules in protein synthesis.
9) How is the number of chromosomes in a gamete different to the number of chromosomes in a fertilised egg?
10) How many DNA bases code for a single amino acid?

Total:

Topic 6 — Inheritance, Variation and Evolution

Mixed Practice Quizzes

Quiz 3 Date: ...... / ...... / ......

1) Where in a cell are proteins synthesised?
2) Give a potential consequence of a mutation in non-coding DNA.
3) What is a genome?
4) How many different DNA bases are there?
5) Which type of reproduction produces offspring that are genetically identical to each other and their parent?
6) Which sex chromosomes does a female have: XY or XX?
7) What is a mutation?
8) Why is the way in which protein chains fold up important?
9) Give two benefits of scientists understanding the complete human genome.
10) What kind of cell division does a fertilised cell undergo to grow into an embryo?

Total:

Quiz 4 Date: ...... / ...... / ......

1) Name the process in which the chromosomes from a male and female gamete get combined.
2) What does a gene code for?
3) True or false? Gametes are formed by mitosis in the reproductive organs.
4) What is the complementary DNA base to C?
5) Describe the shape of a DNA molecule.
6) Explain how a mutation may result in an enzyme no longer working.
7) Describe the structure of a nucleotide.
8) What happens to a cell's genetic information before it starts to divide by meiosis?
9) True or false? Meiosis produces genetically identical cells.
10) Describe how the malaria parasite uses different reproductive methods in different circumstances.

Total:

Genetic Diagrams

Genetic Terms

ALLELE	
DOMINANT	An ⬚ that is always ⬚ .
RECESSIVE	An ⬚ that is only expressed when ⬚ .
HOMOZYGOUS	Both of an organism's alleles for a ⬚ are the ⬚ .
HETEROZYGOUS	An organism's alleles for a ⬚ are ⬚ .
GENOTYPE	
PHENOTYPE	The ⬚ an organism has.

Two Types of Genetic Diagrams

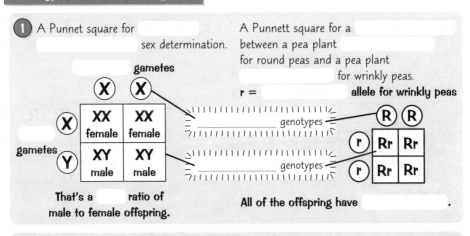

1 A Punnet square for ⬚ ⬚ sex determination.

gametes

gametes

X X

X XX female XX female

Y XY male XY male

That's a ⬚ ratio of male to female offspring.

A Punnett square for a ⬚ between a pea plant ⬚ for round peas and a pea plant ⬚ for wrinkly peas.

r = ⬚ allele for wrinkly peas

⬚ genotypes ⬚ R R

⬚ genotypes ⬚ r Rr Rr

r Rr Rr

All of the offspring have ⬚ .

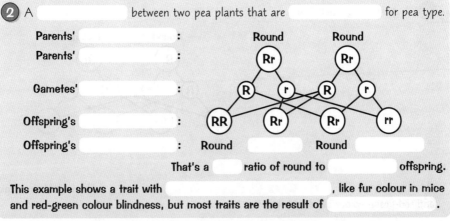

2 A ⬚ between two pea plants that are ⬚ for pea type.

Parents' ⬚	:	Round	Round

Parents' ⬚ : Rr Rr

Gametes' ⬚ : R r R r

Offspring's ⬚ : RR Rr Rr rr

Offspring's ⬚ : Round ⬚ Round ⬚

That's a ⬚ ratio of round to ⬚ offspring.

This example shows a trait with ⬚ , like fur colour in mice and red-green colour blindness, but most traits are the result of ⬚ .

Genetic Diagrams

Genetic Terms

ALLELE	
DOMINANT	
RECESSIVE	
	Both of an organism's alleles for a trait are the same.
	An organism's alleles for a trait are different.
GENOTYPE	
PHENOTYPE	

Two Types of Genetic Diagrams

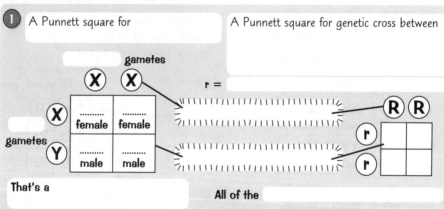

① A Punnett square for

A Punnett square for genetic cross between

.... gametes

r =

	female	female
	male	male

That's a

All of the .

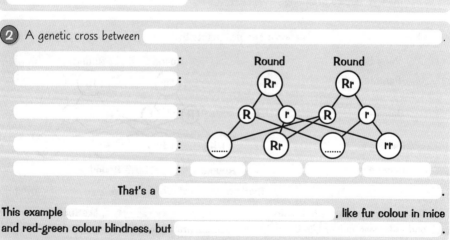

② A genetic cross between .

.... :

.... :

.... :

.... :

.... :

Round   Round

That's a .

This example , like fur colour in mice
and red-green colour blindness, but .

Inherited Disorders

Polydactyly

INHERITED DISORDERS —
disorders caused by ⬚
that are inherited from the ⬚.

POLYDACTYLY — a ⬚
where a baby's born with extra
⬚. It's caused
by a ⬚.

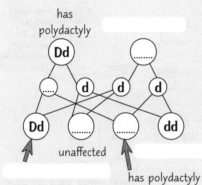

has
polydactyly ⬚

Dd ⬚

(.....) (**d**) (**d**) (**d**)

Dd (.......) (.......) **dd**

unaffected

⬚

has polydactyly

There's a ⬚ % chance of a
⬚ child having the ⬚ if ⬚.

Cystic Fibrosis

CYSTIC FIBROSIS — a genetic disorder
of the ⬚.
It's caused by a ⬚.

A ⬚
is another type
of genetic diagram.

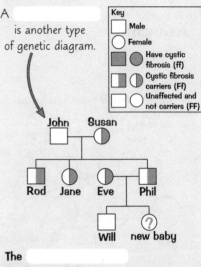

Key
☐ Male
◯ Female
■ ● Have cystic fibrosis (ff)
◨ ◖ Cystic fibrosis carriers (Ff)
☐ ◯ Unaffected and not carriers (FF)

John Susan

Rod Jane Eve Phil

Will new baby (?)

The ⬚
for the new baby are:

● 25% ◖ ⬚ ◯ ⬚

Embryonic Screening

Against Embryonic Screening	For Embryonic Screening
Screening is ⬚.	It will help to stop ⬚.
People might want to screen their embryos so they can pick the ⬚.	Treating disorders costs the ⬚.
It implies that people with genetic problems are '⬚'.	There are ⬚ to stop it going ⬚.

Topic 6 — Inheritance, Variation and Evolution

Inherited Disorders

Polydactyly

INHERITED DISORDERS —

POLYDACTYLY —

has polydactyly   unaffected

Dd   (..........)

(.....) (.....) (.....) (.....)

(.....) (.....) (.....) (.....)

....

....   unaffected

has polydactyly

There's a

if one parent has one D allele.

Cystic Fibrosis

CYSTIC FIBROSIS —

Key

☐ Male

◯ Female

▨ Have cystic fibrosis (ff)

◖ Cystic fibrosis carriers (Ff)

☐ ◖ Unaffected and not carriers (FF)

John   Susan

Rod   Jane   Eve   Phil

Will   new baby

The probabilities

● .... %   ◖ .... %   ◯ .... %

Embryonic Screening

Against Embryonic Screening	For Embryonic Screening
	It will help
People might want	
It implies that	There are

 ✓ ✓ ✓

Developments in Genetics & Variation

Developments in Genetics

Year

1850
- Mendel conducted breeding experiments with _____ .
- Mendel _____

- Scientists became familiar with _____ . They were able to observe how they behaved during _____ .

1900
- Scientists realised there were _____ in the way Mendel's 'units' and _____ acted. It was proposed that the 'units' (_____) were found on the chromosomes.

1950
- Structure of _____ determined.
- Scientists went on to find out _____ .

Three of Mendel's Conclusions

1. _____ 'units' determine _____ .
2. The units are _____ to offspring _____ .
3. The units can be _____ .

Scientists of Mendel's day didn't have the _____ to properly understand _____ .

Variation

VARIATION — differences in the .... of organisms.

Genetic variation
Differences in the _____ individuals inherit cause variation _____ .
This variation is usually _____ .

_____ cause these differences in genes.

E.g. eye colour

	Most mutations	Some mutations	Very few mutations
Effect on phenotype		Slight	New _____

Environmental variation
Differences in the _____ in which an organism develops _____ .

E.g. leaf colour

Genetic and environmental variation
For most characteristics, _____ is caused by both _____ and the _____ .

E.g. plant height

Second Go:
..... /..... /.....

Developments in Genetics & Variation

Developments in Genetics

Year

1850 —

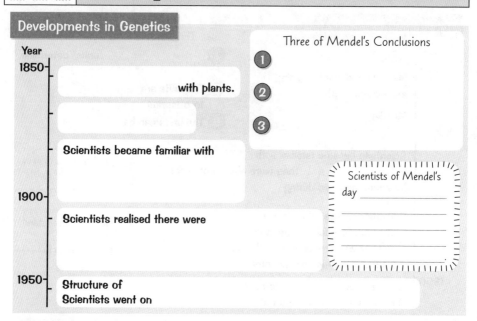

[   ] with plants.

[   ]

Scientists became familiar with

1900 —

Scientists realised there were

1950 — Structure of
Scientists went on

Three of Mendel's Conclusions

1

2

3

Scientists of Mendel's
day _____

Variation

VARIATION — differences ....

Genetic variation

Differences in the

This variation is

Mutations cause

E.g. _____

	Most mutations	Some mutations	Very few mutations
Effect on phenotype			

Environmental variation

Differences in the

E.g. _____

Genetic and environmental variation

For most characteristics,

E.g. _____

Topic 6 — Inheritance, Variation and Evolution

Evolution and Speciation

Charles Darwin

Best known for: the theory of
_____ .
Published: _____
_____ (1859)
Controversy: the theory
_____ some _____ ideas.
Research: a world expedition, _____ ,
discussions, knowledge of _____ .
Setbacks: _____
to convince many scientists because the
_____ wasn't known about.

Alfred Russel Wallace

Best known for:
work on _____
_____ in
animals and his theory
of _____ .
Published: joint writings with
_____ on evolution (_____)
Research: observations from
_____ provided
evidence for the _____
_____ by natural selection.

Natural Selection

The theory of evolution: All of _____ have evolved from
_____ that first started to develop over _____ years ago.

Species show
....
.... Organisms with the → These organisms are
....
....
Limited resources → .... The beneficial characteristics
mean organisms are in for the environment are are passed on and
.... more likely to survive. gradually become ....
.... in the population.

Jean-Baptiste Lamarck argued that changes acquired during an _____
were passed on to its _____ , but _____ didn't support this hypothesis.

Speciation

SPECIATION — the development of a _____ by _____ .

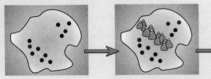 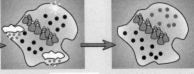

_____
of a species.

Populations are
_____ .

Populations _____
to new environments.

Development of
_____ .

Two groups become _____ when individuals have changed so much
that they won't be able to _____ with one another to produce _____ .

Second Go:
..... /..... /.....

Evolution and Speciation

Charles Darwin

Best known for:

Published:

Controversy:

Research:

Setbacks:

Alfred Russel Wallace

Best known for:

Published:

Research:

Natural Selection

The theory of evolution:

Limited resources

Organisms with the

The beneficial characteristics

Jean-Baptiste Lamarck argued

Speciation

SPECIATION —

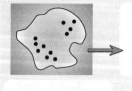

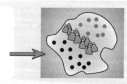

Populations are isolated.

Development of

Two groups become separate species when individuals have changed so much that they

Topic 6 — Inheritance, Variation and Evolution

Mixed Practice Quizzes

Time for some more quiz questions now folks. These quizzes are based on p.99-106 so get ready to test your knowledge of genetics, variation and evolution.

Quiz 1   Date: ...... / ...... / ......

1) What is polydactyly? ☐
2) Which scientist is most well known for his work on warning colouration in animals? ☐
3) What is the theory of evolution by natural selection? ☐
4) What is an allele? ☐
5) What kind of experiments did Mendel carry out? ☐
6) True or false? Genetic variation within a species is usually extensive. ☐
7) What was Darwin's book on evolution by natural selection called? ☐
8) Give three arguments against embryonic screening for inherited disorders. ☐
9) In a genetic diagram, does an upper case letter usually represent a dominant or recessive allele? ☐
10) When would two isolated populations be considered separate species? ☐

Total: ☐

Quiz 2   Date: ...... / ...... / ......

1) What are inherited disorders caused by? ☐
2) What is variation? ☐
3) Is the allele that causes cystic fibrosis recessive or dominant? ☐
4) What causes environmental variation within a population? ☐
5) What do the letters written above and alongside a Punnett square represent? ☐
6) Give an example of a characteristic that is controlled by a single gene. ☐
7) Why was 'On the Origin of Species' controversial when it was published? ☐
8) What are Mendel's hereditary 'units' known as today? ☐
9) How long ago did the simple life forms that all living species evolved from first start to develop? ☐
10) True or false? Differences in genes are caused by mutations. ☐

Total: ☐

Mixed Practice Quizzes

Quiz 3   Date: ...... / ...... / ......

1) What does homozygous mean?
2) In what year was 'On the Origin of Species' published?
3) True or false? A dominant allele is always expressed.
4) In which century was the behaviour of chromosomes during cell division first observed?
5) What is cystic fibrosis?
6) True or false? Variation in characteristics is only caused by genes.
7) How did Jean-Baptiste Lamarck believe that species evolved?
8) What is an organism's phenotype?
9) Give three arguments for embryonic screening for inherited disorders.
10) Are most characteristics caused by a single gene or multiple genes interacting?

Total:

Quiz 4   Date: ...... / ...... / ......

1) What is speciation?
2) If an organism has two different alleles for a trait, is the organism heterozygous or homozygous for that trait?
3) True or false? Polydactyly is caused by a dominant allele.
4) Which two scientists published joint writings on evolution in 1858?
5) What is an organism's genotype?
6) In which century was the structure of DNA determined?
7) What is Charles Darwin best known for?
8) How many copies of a recessive allele need to be present for it to be expressed?
9) Why were Mendel's discoveries not really understood until after his death?
10) True or false? Mutations often result in a new phenotype.

Total:

Topic 6 — Inheritance, Variation and Evolution

Uses of Genetics

Selective Breeding

SELECTIVE BREEDING — breeding plants or animals for [____].

Four uses of selective breeding:

1 Greater [____] production.

2 Big or unusual [____].

3 A good, gentle [____] in dogs.

4 [____] in crops.

Individuals with [____] bred together.

Repeated over [____]

Humans have used selective breeding for [____].

However, it can lead to [____].

Four Types of Cloning

1 Embryo [____]

2 [____] culture

3 [____]

4 [____] cloning

Used to clone [____].

[____] cell

[____] removed

+

[____] cell

[____] removed

makes it divide

[____]

(with same genes as adult body cell)

embryo implanted into

[____]

Genetic Engineering

Genetic engineering transfers a [____] responsible for a [____] from one organism's genome into another organism. Three uses of genetic engineering:

1 Genes for producing [____] [____] transferred to bacteria.

2 Genes for [____] fruit transferred to crops.

3 Genes for resistance to [____] transferred to crops.

[____] gene

gene cut out with [____]

gene inserted into [____]

vector introduced to the [____]

Pros of GM crops	Cons of GM crops
	Could reduce
Helps people with diets that lack nutrients	Concerns about
Already being grown	may spread into the wild

Topic 6 — Inheritance, Variation and Evolution

Uses of Genetics

Selective Breeding

SELECTIVE BREEDING —

Four uses of selective breeding:
1
2
3
4

Individuals with

Humans have used
....
....
However, ...
....

Four Types of Cloning

1
2
3
4

electric shock makes it divide

Genetic Engineering

Genetic engineering transfers

Three uses of genetic engineering:
1
2
3

vector introduced
to the

Pros of GM crops:	Cons of GM crops:

Fossils and Antibiotic Resistance

Fossils

FOSSILS — remains of organisms from

Three ways that fossils form:

1. Gradual replacement by   — happens to   .

2.   — e.g. footprints, burrows and rootlet traces.

3. Preservation — in places where conditions   , parts of organisms can be   .

Fossils show   organisms have changed as   but there's uncertainty over how life began because the   :

> Many early forms of life were   and   .

> Some fossils have been destroyed by   .

> Studying fossils and antibiotic-resistant bacteria contributed to the
> ....
> being widely accepted.

Antibiotic-Resistant Bacteria

Bacteria can   because they   .

> .... is a type of antibiotic-resistant bacterium.

can lead to resistance to an antibiotic.

Resistant bacteria survive the   and   .

Populations of resistant bacteria arise and   , because people aren't   and there isn't   .

Developing new antibiotics is   , and is unlikely to keep up with the   .

Three ways to reduce the rate of development of antibiotic-resistant strains:

1. Not prescribing antibiotics for   infections.

2. Reducing the use of antibiotics in   .

3. Patients taking the   to kill all the bacteria.

> Any bacteria not   might develop into   .

 ☑   ☑   ☑

Fossils and Antibiotic Resistance

Second Go:
..... /..... /.....

Fossils

FOSSILS —

Three ways that fossils form:

1

2

3 Preservation —

Fossils show how

is incomplete:

Many early forms of life were

Some fossils have been

Studying fossils and antibiotic-resistant bacteria

....

....

....

Antibiotic-Resistant Bacteria

Bacteria can

.... is a type of

....

....

Resistant bacteria

Populations of resistant bacteria

to an antibiotic.

Developing new antibiotics is

Three ways to reduce the rate of development of antibiotic-resistant strains:

1

2

3

Any bacteria not .... might develop into ....

Topic 6 — Inheritance, Variation and Evolution

Classification and Extinction

The Linnaean System

The Linnaean system was developed by _____ .

It organises organisms by their _____

_____ into these groups.

Kingdom

_____

Class

_____

Family

_____

_____ system

Genus _____

E.g. *Homo sapiens*

Developments in Classification

_____ showed us more about _____ of organisms.

Improved chemical analysis increased our understanding of _____ .

New models of _____ proposed, e.g. Carl Woese's _____ .

Bacteria	
Archaea	a different type of _____ usually found in extreme places
Eukaryota	including protists, _____

Evolutionary Trees

Evolutionary trees show how scientists think _____ are _____ .

_____

_____

ancestor

ancestor

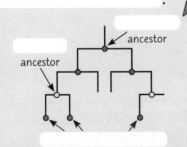

_____

Data source	Living species	Extinct species
	Current _____ data	Fossil data

Extinction

EXTINCTION — when _____ of a _____ .

_____ change

New _____

New _____

_____

_____ events

Classification and Extinction

The Linnaean System

The Linnaean system

It organises organisms

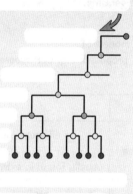

E.g. *Homo*   *sapiens*

Developments in Classification

Better microscopes showed us more about

Improved chemical analysis

New models of

Bacteria	
Archaea	
Eukaryota	

Evolutionary Trees

Evolutionary trees

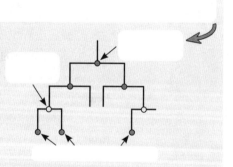

	Living species	Extinct species
Data source		

Extinction

EXTINCTION —

Mixed Practice Quizzes

Have a go at the following quizzes to see if you could be classified as a biology genius. All the questions are based on what you can remember from p.109-114.

Quiz 1
Date: ...... / ...... / ......

1) What are fossils?
2) What is used to cut out a desired gene in genetic engineering?
3) How have better microscopes led to developments in classification?
4) Give a useful substance that genetically engineered bacterial cells can be used to produce.
5) Give two reasons why the fossil record is incomplete.
6) Give one problem that can be caused by selective breeding.
7) Who proposed the three domain system of classification?
8) Give three ways to reduce the rate of development of antibiotic-resistant strains of bacteria.
9) Why is an electric shock used in adult cell cloning?
10) What is a vector used for in genetic engineering?

Total:

Quiz 2
Date: ...... / ...... / ......

1) What is extinction?
2) Give four groups of organisms within Eukaryota.
3) What do evolutionary trees show?
4) Give one benefit and one risk of GM crops.
5) True or false? Fossils and antibiotic-resistant bacteria are used as evidence for the theory of evolution by natural selection.
6) Give four types of cloning.
7) What is used to organise organisms in the Linnaean system?
8) Why are bacteria able to evolve quickly?
9) Give four characteristics that selective breeding can be used to improve.
10) Describe the process of adult cell cloning.

Total:

Mixed Practice Quizzes

Date: ...... / ...... / ......

1) What is selective breeding?
2) Give three ways that fossils can form.
3) Describe the steps involved in genetic engineering.
4) Name an antibiotic-resistant strain of bacteria.
5) Looking at the fossil record, why is it difficult to be certain how life began?
6) In the binomial name of a species what comes first: genus or species?
7) Give the seven levels of classification used in the Linnaean system.
8) Give the three domains of the three domain system of classification.
9) Give five factors that can cause extinction.
10) Give two reasons why antibiotic-resistant bacteria are able to spread so easily.

Total:

Quiz 4   Date: ...... / ...... / ......

1) Who developed the Linnaean system?
2) What is genetic engineering?
3) What type of organisms are archaea?
4) How does antibiotic resistance arise in a population of bacteria?
5) How have improvements in chemical analysis led to developments in classification?
6) True or false? The live animal produced from adult cell cloning will have different genes to the adult body cell it was cloned from.
7) Give three examples of traces of organisms that can be preserved as casts or impressions.
8) Describe the process of selective breeding.
9) Give two types of data used to produce evolutionary trees.
10) Explain why it is important to finish a course of antibiotics.

Total:

Basics of Ecology

First Go:
..... /..... /.....

Definitions of Ecological Terms

	All the organisms of one species living in a habitat.
COMMUNITY	
STABLE COMMUNITY	A community in which all species and environmental factors are in ....
ECOSYSTEM	The interaction of a community of ....
	A feature that enables an organism to survive in the conditions of its normal habitat.
	Each species in a community depending upon other species for things, e.g. ...., food, shelter or seed dispersal.

Due to ...., change in an ecosystem (e.g. ....) can affect the whole community.

Factors Affecting Communities

Both .... (living) and .... (non-living) factors can affect organisms in a community:

Light intensity

Wind and ....

.... (for plants)

.... level

Competition

Organisms compete for: light, ..., minerals, ..., food, ...,

New ....

Food availability

Temperature

.... (for aquatic animals)

New pathogens

Soil .... and ....

One species may .... another so that numbers are ....

Three Types of Adaptation

1 Structural   2 ....   3 ....

.... — organisms that are adapted to live in extreme conditions, such as ...., high pressure or high salt concentration (e.g. ....).

118

Basics of Ecology

Definitions of Ecological Terms

POPULATION:

COMMUNITY:

STABLE COMMUNITY: A community in which

ECOSYSTEM:

ADAPTATION:

INTERDEPENDENCE:

Due to _____, change in an
ecosystem _____

Factors Affecting Communities

_____ factors can
affect organisms in a community:

intensity

Organisms compete for:

Competition

Temperature

O_2 level

One species may _____

Three Types of Adaptation

1

2

3

EXTREMOPHILES —

Food Chains & Environmental Change

Food Chains

CONSUMER   CONSUMER

— a plant or [____]
that makes glucose by
[____].

All food chains start
with a [____].

— an animal that eats
[____] and
may be eaten by
[____].

— an animal that eats
[____]
and may be eaten by
[____].

[____] — a consumer that kills and eats other animals ([____]).

BIOMASS — [____].

[____] stored in biomass is transferred along food chains and used by
other organisms to [____].

Predator-Prey Cycles

In a [____] the
numbers of predators and prey rise and
fall in cycles:

 Prey population
increases

Predator
population
[____]

[____]

Prey population
decreases

Predator-prey cycles are always out of
phase with each other, as it
[____]

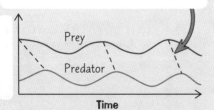

Prey

Predator

Time

Environmental Changes

Environmental changes can cause the
[____]
to change.

Three examples of these
environmental changes are:

1 Water availability
— e.g. how much
[____] there is.

2 [____]

3 Atmospheric gases
— e.g. how much [____]
there is.

Changes can be caused by seasonal
factors, [____]
factors or [____]
[____].

Food Chains & Environmental Change

Food Chains

PREDATOR —

BIOMASS —

_____ is transferred along food chains and

_____ .

Predator-Prey Cycles

In a _____ the numbers of predators and prey rise and fall in cycles:

Prey population increases

Predator-prey cycles are always

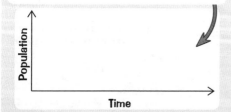

Environmental Changes

Environmental changes can cause

Three examples of these environmental changes are:

1

2

3

Changes can be caused by

....
....
....

Topic 7 — Ecology

Cycling of Materials

Recycling Materials

Materials are cycled through the [____] and [____] parts of an ecosystem.

[____], absorption from [____]

Materials in the ⟶ Materials in

[____] ⟵ [____]

[____], death and decay

Materials decay because they're broken down by [____].
Decay puts materials like [____] back into the soil.

The Water Cycle

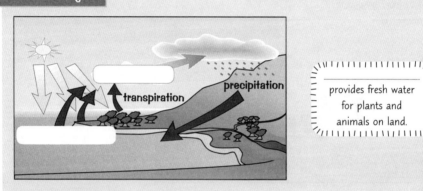

transpiration   precipitation

[____] provides fresh water for plants and animals on land.

The Carbon Cycle

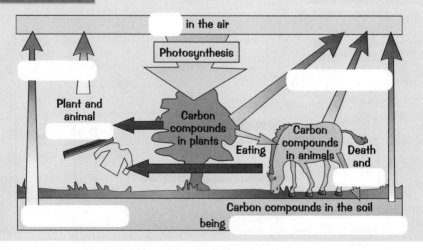

[____] in the air

Photosynthesis

Plant and animal [____]

Carbon compounds in plants

Eating

Carbon compounds in animals

Death and [____]

Carbon compounds in the soil

being [____]

Topic 7 — Ecology

Cycling of Materials

Recycling Materials

Materials are cycled through the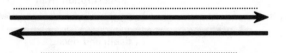

Materials decay because
Decay puts

The Water Cycle

The Carbon Cycle

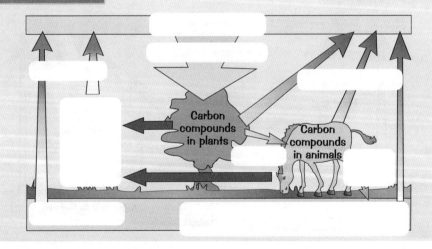

Carbon
compounds
in plants

Carbon
compounds
in animals

Decay and Biodiversity

Three Factors that Increase the Rate of Decay

1 [ ] temperatures **2** Plenty of [ ] **3** [ ] conditions

Farmers and gardeners provide ideal
conditions for decay when making compost
([ ]
[ ]).

These three things create ideal
conditions for _____

Biogas

Biogas is produced by [ ]

It's mainly made up of [ ],
which can be [ ]
[ ].

Biogas is made on a large scale
from waste material (e.g. [ ]
[ ])
in biogas generators.

Inlet for waste
material

Gas

Waste material and [ ]

Outlet for
digested material
(used as [ ])

Biodiversity

BIODIVERSITY — [ ]

[ ]
(lots of different species) ⟹ of one species on another for
things like [ ] , [ ]
and the maintenance of the
[ ] . ⟹ [ ]

For [ ]
[ ] , it's
important that a good level of
biodiversity is maintained.

Sadly, _____
_____ — we've only
recently started taking measures to stop this.

Second Go:
..... / ..... / .....

Decay and Biodiversity

Three Factors that Increase the Rate of Decay

1   **2**   **3**

provide ideal conditions for decay when
making _____ (

).

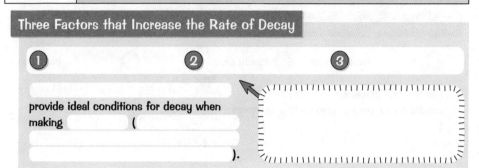

Biogas

Biogas is produced by

It's mainly made

Biogas is made on a large scale

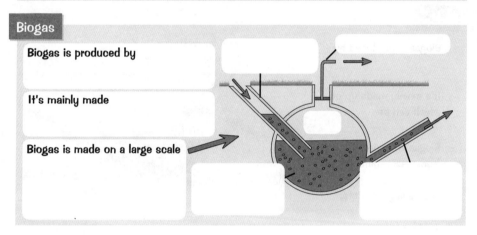

Biodiversity

BIODIVERSITY —

Reduced dependence

**For the human species to
survive,**

Sadly,

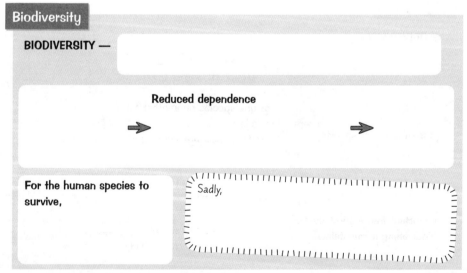

Mixed Practice Quizzes

Predator-prey, water, carbon — there have been so many cycles on pages 117-124 that you might be feeling dizzy, but it's not over yet... Onwards to the quizzes.

Quiz 1

Date: ...... / ...... / ......

1) In the water cycle, what happens after rising water cools and condenses?

2) Give four examples of things that species in a community might depend upon other species for.

3) Why are predator-prey cycles always out of phase with each other?

4) What is compost?

5) Give three things that animals compete for.

6) How is carbon taken out of the air in the carbon cycle?

7) What are secondary consumers?

8) What type of decay produces biogas?

9) What are the three types of adaptation organisms may have?

10) True or false? Decay is caused by microorganisms.

Total:

Quiz 2

Date: ...... / ...... / ......

1) What is the difference between a population and a community?

2) Give one use of biogas.

3) How does high biodiversity lead to stable ecosystems?

4) Give a material that microorganisms involved in decay return to the soil.

5) Describe what might happen to the population of a species when it is outcompeted by another species.

6) True or false? Low temperatures increase the rate of decay.

7) Give four biotic factors that can affect organisms in a community.

8) Apart from biogas production, give one way in which the decay process is exploited for human use.

9) Give one reason why maintaining a good level of biodiversity is important.

10) What is meant by 'anaerobic decay'?

Total:

Mixed Practice Quizzes

Quiz 3   Date: ...... / ...... / ......

1) Give an example of an extremophile.
2) Give seven abiotic factors that can affect organisms in a community.
3) Which gas is biogas mainly made up of?
4) How are carbon compounds in plants transferred to other parts of the carbon cycle?
5) Which stage of the water cycle provides fresh water for organisms on land?
6) What process is carried out by all producers, but not consumers?
7) What is a tertiary consumer?
8) Define 'ecosystem'.
9) List four things that plants compete for.
10) Give three examples of environmental changes that can cause the distribution of organisms to change.

Total:

Quiz 4   Date: ...... / ...... / ......

1) List three ways that carbon compounds in animals are transferred to other parts of the carbon cycle.
2) How does burning fossil fuels affect the CO_2 concentration of the air?
3) Give two types of organisms that can be producers.
4) What is the definition of a 'stable community'?
5) Define 'biodiversity'.
6) Give two types of factors that can cause environmental changes.
7) What term describes organisms that are adapted to live in extreme conditions?
8) Give two abiotic factors regarding the soil that may affect organisms in a community.
9) List three things that create ideal conditions for organisms involved in decay.
10) What is biomass?

Total:

Human Effects on Ecosystems

Global Warming

The Earth is gradually heating up as a result of

Three consequences of global warming could be:

trapped

greenhouse gases
(e.g.   and   )

1 Rising sea levels (so   ).

2 A change in the   of some organisms.

3 A decrease in   (as some species may become extinct).

Land Use and Deforestation

Humans use land for things like   ,   ,   and
                        . This means there's

PEAT BOG DESTRUCTION

peat bog

bog
drained

peat sold as

and

release   into
the atmosphere

peat sold
as

                        for different
animals, plants and
microorganisms

                        — the cutting down of forests.

It has been done on a large-scale in   areas in order to:

- clear land for   and   ,

- grow crops to make   .

Human Effects on Ecosystems

Global Warming

The Earth is _____
as a result of _____
_____
_____ .

Three consequences of global warming could be:

 1 _____

 2 _____

 3 _____

Land Use and Deforestation

Humans use land for things like _____

This means _____

PEAT BOG DESTRUCTION

peat bog

bog

_____ — the cutting down of forests.

It has been done on _____ in order to:

- _____
- _____

Maintaining Ecosystems

Pollution

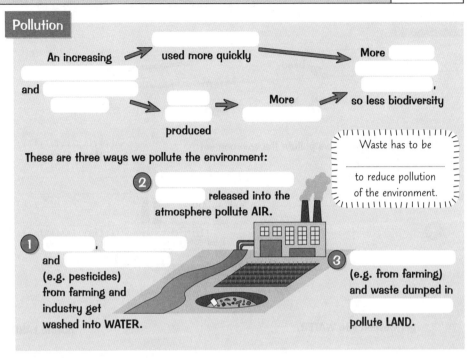

An increasing [ ] used more quickly [ ] More [ ]

and [ ]

[ ] produced More [ ] so less biodiversity

These are three ways we pollute the environment:

Waste has to be
_____
to reduce pollution
of the environment.

2 [ ] released into the
atmosphere pollute AIR.

1 [ ], [ ]
and [ ]
(e.g. pesticides)
from farming and
industry get
washed into WATER.

3 [ ]
(e.g. from farming)
and waste dumped in
[ ]
pollute LAND.

Five Programmes to Protect Ecosystems

1 [ ] programmes —
[ ] species are [ ]
[ ] to make sure the species survive.

Programmes like these are set
up to reduce the _____
_____
_____.

2 Habitat restoration — rare habitats like
[ ], [ ] and [ ]
[ ] are protected and regenerated.

3 [ ] —
these are reintroduced around fields where only a single crop type
is grown, creating [ ].

4 Government regulations — e.g. [ ]
[ ].

5 [ ] — reduces the amount of waste going to landfill sites.

Topic 7 — Ecology

Maintaining Ecosystems

Pollution

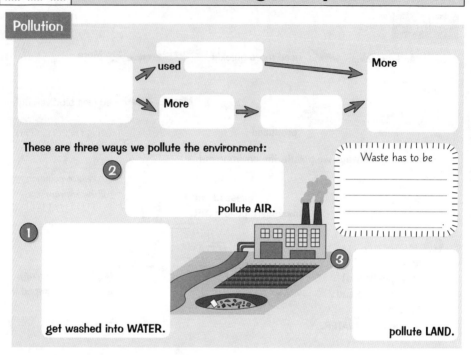

These are three ways we pollute the environment:

Waste has to be
_____
_____
_____
_____

② _____ pollute AIR.

① _____ get washed into WATER.

③ _____ pollute LAND.

Five Programmes to Protect Ecosystems

Programmes like these are
set up _____
_____
_____
_____

① Breeding programmes — _____

② _____ — _____
_____ are protected and regenerated.

③ Hedgerows and field margins — _____

④ _____ — e.g. to reduce deforestation
and _____ .

⑤ _____ — reduces the amount of _____
_____ .

Trophic Levels

Trophic Levels and Biomass

TROPHIC LEVEL — [_____].

[_____] — a diagram showing the relative amounts of biomass at each trophic level.

Carnivores with no predators are called [_____].

Trophic level 4: carnivore ← [_____] consumer

Trophic level 3: carnivore Secondary consumer

Trophic level 2: [_____] Primary consumer

Trophic level 1: plants/[_____] [_____]

Decomposers (e.g. [_____]) secrete [_____] to break down dead plant and animal matter into small [_____] food molecules. These then [_____] into the microorganisms.

Biomass Transfer

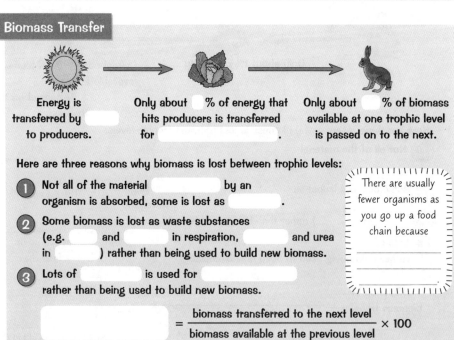

Energy is transferred by [_____] to producers.

Only about [___]% of energy that hits producers is transferred for [_____].

Only about [___]% of biomass available at one trophic level is passed on to the next.

Here are three reasons why biomass is lost between trophic levels:

1. Not all of the material [_____] by an organism is absorbed, some is lost as [_____].

2. Some biomass is lost as waste substances (e.g. [___] and [_____] in respiration, [_____] and urea in [_____]) rather than being used to build new biomass.

3. Lots of [_____] is used for [_____] rather than being used to build new biomass.

There are usually fewer organisms as you go up a food chain because [_____]

$$[\text{_____}] = \frac{\text{biomass transferred to the next level}}{\text{biomass available at the previous level}} \times 100$$

Topic 7 — Ecology

Trophic Levels

Trophic Levels and Biomass

TROPHIC LEVEL —

PYRAMID OF BIOMASS —

Carnivores with no _____ are called _____

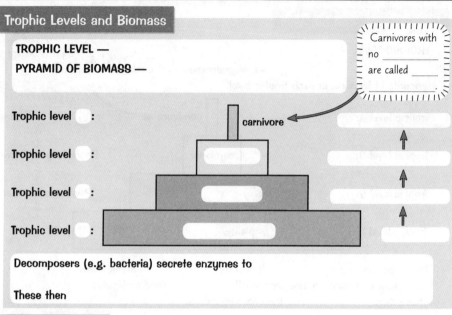

Trophic level ( ):

Trophic level ( ):

Trophic level ( ):

Trophic level ( ):

carnivore

Decomposers (e.g. bacteria) secrete enzymes to

These then

Biomass Transfer

Only about 1% of energy

Only about ( ) % of biomass available at one _____ is passed on to the next.

Here are three reasons why biomass is lost between trophic levels:

1 Not all of the material

2 Some biomass is lost as _____ (e.g. _____ , water and _____ in _____) rather than being used to build new biomass.

3 Lots of _____ rather than being used to build new biomass.

There are usually _____ as you go up a food chain because _____

efficiency of biomass transfer = —————————— × ....
....

Food Security and Biotechnology

Food Security Threats

FOOD SECURITY —

It's threatened by these six things:

1 Increasing

2 _____ in developed
countries (meaning they take scarce
food resources from other countries).

3 New _____
that affect crops and livestock.

4 Environmental changes that affect farming
(e.g. changes in _____).

5 Cost of farming

6

_of food production are
needed to feed everyone
now and in the future._

Increasing Efficiency

Food can be _____

by reducing the energy
transferred from livestock to

_____ ,

for example:

• by restricting ....

• by keeping animals in
....
....
....

....
food can also be fed to
animals to increase growth.

Overfishing

Fish stocks are _____ due to overfishing. We need to maintain stocks
at a level where the fish _____ . This can be done by:

Introducing _____   Controlling _____

Biotechnology

BIOTECHNOLOGY —

It can be used to produce food for the growing human population
(e.g. microorganisms can be cultured for use as a food source).

Glucose syrup
+   conditions →   fungal   harvesting and →   _____ —
Fusarium fungus   biomass   used to make protein-rich
food (suitable for
_____)

_____ crops can produce
more food or food with a greater nutritional value —
e.g. '_____' produces a chemical that's
converted into vitamin A in the body.

_Human _____ can
be produced by genetically
engineered bacteria._

Second Go:
..... /..... /.....

Food Security and Biotechnology

Food Security Threats

FOOD SECURITY —

It's threatened by these six things:

1.

2. Changing

3. New

4. Environmental

5. Cost of

6.

Increasing Efficiency

Food can be produced more efficiently by

,

for example:

- by restricting ....
- by keeping animals in
  ....
  ....
  ....

....
....
.... to increase growth.

Overfishing

_____ due to overfishing. We need to maintain
_____ .

This can be done by:

Biotechnology

BIOTECHNOLOGY —

It can be used to produce food for the _____ human population
(e.g. _____ can be _____ for use as a food source).

....   fungal   ....   Mycoprotein — ....
+   ....   biomass   ....
Fusarium fungus →   ....

_____ crops can produce more
food or food with a
— e.g. 'golden rice' produces a

.... can be
.... produced by ....

Topic 7 — Ecology

Mixed Practice Quizzes

Don't let any of this precious revision time go to waste — work your way through
these quizzes covering pages 127-134 and see how many you can get right.

Quiz 1

Date: ...... / ...... / ......

1) How does recycling protect ecosystems?
2) What is food security?
3) Describe two ways that toxic chemicals pollute the natural environment.
4) What is a trophic level?
5) Give two reasons why deforestation is happening in tropical areas.
6) Why are there usually fewer organisms as you go up a food chain?
7) What type of fungus is used to make mycoprotein?
8) Besides fungus, what else is required to produce mycoprotein?
9) Give two ways that government regulations could protect ecosystems.
10) What do decomposers do?

Total:

Quiz 2

Date: ...... / ...... / ......

1) What is happening to fish stocks, and why?
2) What does a pyramid of biomass show?
3) How does the use of peat for fuel have an environmental impact?
4) Explain two ways in which global warming could affect organisms.
5) During mycoprotein production, is fungus grown in aerobic or
   anaerobic conditions?
6) How do breeding programmes help to protect biodiversity?
7) Give three waste substances that animals lose some biomass as.
8) Give one way that environmental change could be a threat to food security.
9) Give two ways that the amount of energy transferred from
   livestock to the environment can be reduced?
10) How can human insulin be produced using biotechnology?

Total:

Mixed Practice Quizzes

Quiz 3 Date: ...... / ...... / ......

1) How has the increase in the standard of living resulted in more pollution? ☑
2) What percentage of the energy that hits producers is transferred for photosynthesis? ☑
3) Give two things that peat is sold for. ☑
4) Besides controlling net size, give one way humans can maintain fish stocks. ☑
5) Programmes that protect and regenerate rare habitats are an example of programmes set up to maintain what? ☑
6) What are apex predators? ☑
7) Approximately what percentage of biomass available at one trophic level is passed on to the next? ☑
8) Which trophic level are primary consumers found at? ☑
9) Why might high-protein food be fed to livestock? ☑
10) Give two uses of biotechnology that help feed the growing population. ☑

Total:

Quiz 4 Date: ...... / ...... / ......

1) Increasing atmospheric levels of what are causing the Earth to warm up? ☑
2) Why have farmers reintroduced hedgerows and field margins in some areas? ☑
3) List four activities that humans commonly use land for. ☑
4) How does respiration contribute to the loss of biomass between trophic levels? ☑
5) Give three ways that water is polluted. ☑
6) How do decomposers break down dead plant and animal matter? ☑
7) Why do changing diets in developed countries threaten food security? ☑
8) List five other threats to food security. ☑
9) What is mycoprotein? ☑
10) How is 'golden rice' different from other rice? ☑

Total:

Required Practicals 1

Microscopy

Start with the [____] lens then move the stage up with the [____] adjustment knob.

Look down the [____] and adjust the [____] with the adjustment knobs (use the coarse one first).

To see the slide with a greater [____], swap to a higher-powered lens and [____].

When drawing your observations:
- use a [____]
- draw [____] lines
- [____] important features
- include a [____].

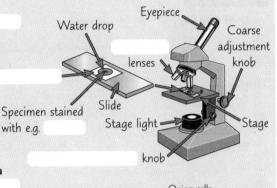

Eyepiece
Water drop
Coarse adjustment knob
[____] lenses
Slide
Specimen stained with e.g. [____]
Stage light
Stage
[____] knob

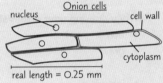

Onion cells
nucleus
cell wall
cytoplasm
real length = 0.25 mm
magnification = × 100

Osmosis

Four steps to investigate the effect of [____] of sugar or salt solutions on plant tissue:

1. Cut a potato into [____] cylinders.

2. [____] of each cylinder.

3. Prepare beakers containing different concentrations of sugar or salt solution and one of [____]. Put one cylinder in each beaker.

4. Leave for 24 hours and then take out the cylinders and [____] [____]. Measure their masses again.

$$\% \text{ change in mass} = \frac{\text{new mass} - \text{original mass}}{[\_\_\_\_]} \times [\_\_\_\_]$$

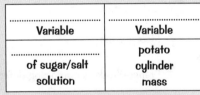

Potato cylinder
[____] or sugar/salt solution

.... Variable	.... Variable
.... of sugar/salt solution	potato cylinder mass

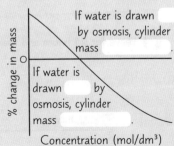

If water is drawn [____] by osmosis, cylinder mass [____].

If water is drawn [____] by osmosis, cylinder mass [____].

% change in mass

Concentration (mol/dm³)

Second Go: ..... /..... /.....	**Required Practicals 1**

Microscopy

Start with the

Look down the

To see the

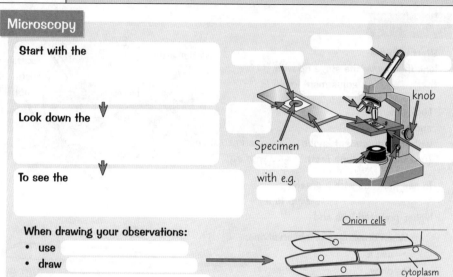

knob

Specimen

with e.g.

When drawing your observations:
- use
- draw
- •
- include a

<u>Onion cells</u>

cytoplasm

real length = 0.25 mm

magnification = × 100

Osmosis

Four steps to investigate the effect of

1. Cut a potato

2. Measure the

3. Prepare beakers containing different

4. Leave for 24 hours and then

Independent Variable	Dependent Variable

If water is

_____, cylinder

mass _____.

If water is

_____, cylinder

mass _____.

(mol/dm³)

$$\boxed{} = \frac{\boxed{}\ \text{mass} - \boxed{}\ \text{mass}}{\boxed{}} \times 100$$

 ✓ ✓ ✓

Required Practicals 2

Antibiotics and Bacterial Growth

Five steps to prepare an _____ culture of bacteria in a lab:

1 A Petri dish and some _____ jelly are _____ (e.g. heated to a high temperature) to kill any _____ in them.

2 Hot agar jelly is poured into the Petri dish and allowed to _____.

3 An _____ loop is passed through a hot flame to _____ it.

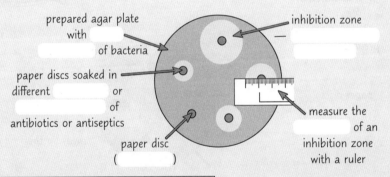

Petri dish

agar jelly

4 The _____ is used to _____ to the agar jelly.

5 The Petri dish is _____ to stop microorganisms in the air getting in. It is stored at 25 °C and upside down to _____.

prepared agar plate with _____ of bacteria

paper discs soaked in different _____ or _____ of antibiotics or antiseptics

paper disc (_____)

inhibition zone ___ _____

measure the _____ of an inhibition zone with a ruler

Independent Variable	Dependent Variable
	width of inhibition zone

More effective antibiotic/ _____ ⟹ _____ inhibition zone

area of inhibition zone = _____

one _____

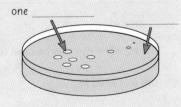

The equation can also be used to calculate the area of a _____. You just need to measure the _____ of the _____ you're interested in.

Required Practicals 2

Antibiotics and Bacterial Growth

Five steps to prepare _____ :

1 A Petri dish and some

2 Hot agar jelly

3 An inoculating

4 The inoculating

5 The Petri dish is

It is stored at

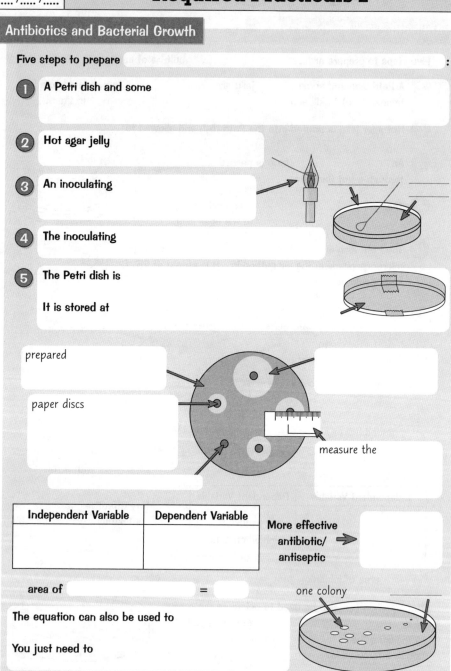

prepared

paper discs

measure the

Independent Variable	Dependent Variable

More effective
antibiotic/
antiseptic

area of _____ = _____

one colony

The equation can also be used to

You just need to

Required Practicals 3

Effect of pH on Amylase Activity

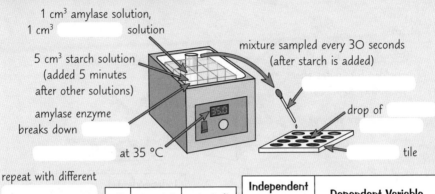

1 cm³ amylase solution,
1 cm³ _____ solution

5 cm³ starch solution
(added 5 minutes
after other solutions)

amylase enzyme
breaks down _____

_____ at 35 °C

mixture sampled every 30 seconds
(after starch is added)

drop of _____

_____ tile

repeat with different _____

record time
when iodine
solution remains
_____
after sample
is added

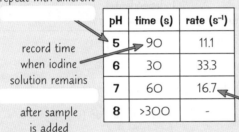

pH	time (s)	rate (s⁻¹)
5	90	11.1
6	30	33.3
7	60	16.7
8	>300	-

Independent Variable	Dependent Variable
.... of solution	time taken for ....

$$\text{Rate of reaction ( )} = \frac{1000}{\text{time (s)}}$$

Food Tests

Test	Method	Positive result
Benedict's test (for ....)	Add about .... drops of Benedict's solution to a 5 cm³ food sample and leave for 5 minutes at .... °C.	.... → .... yellow brick red
.... test (for starch)	Add a few drops of .... solution to a 5 cm³ food sample and mix.	.... - .... → blue-black
Biuret test (for ....)	Add 2 cm³ of biuret solution to a 2 cm³ food sample and mix.	blue → ....
.... test (for ....)	Add 3 drops of .... stain solution to a 5 cm³ food sample and mix.	Mixture separates into two layers — ....

Required Practicals 3

Effect of pH on Amylase Activity

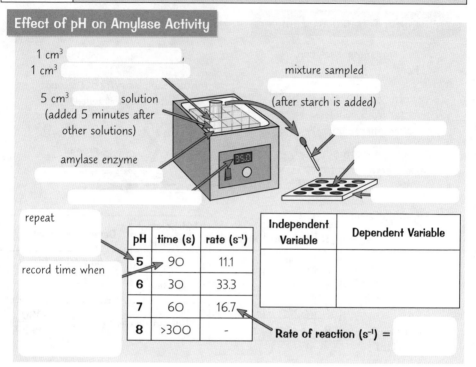

1 cm³ _____ ,
1 cm³ _____

5 cm³ _____ solution
(added 5 minutes after
other solutions)

amylase enzyme

mixture sampled
(after starch is added)

repeat _____

record time when _____

pH	time (s)	rate (s⁻¹)
5	90	11.1
6	30	33.3
7	60	16.7
8	>300	-

Independent Variable	Dependent Variable

Rate of reaction (s⁻¹) = _____

Food Tests

Test	Method	Positive result
_____ test (for _____)	Add about 10 drops of Benedict's solution to a 5 cm³ food sample and _____	blue
(for starch)		
Biuret test (for _____)	Add _____ to a 2 cm³ food sample and mix.	
	Add _____ of Sudan III stain solution to a 5 cm³ food sample and mix.	

Required Practicals 4

Effect of Light Intensity on Photosynthesis Rate

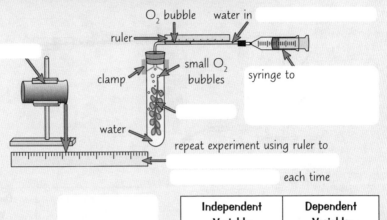

O₂ bubble   water in [____]

ruler

clamp   small O₂ bubbles   syringe to

water

repeat experiment using ruler to [____]

each time

$$\text{Rate (cm/min)} = \frac{\boxed{}}{\text{time (min)}}$$

Independent Variable	Dependent Variable
distance from light	

[____] light intensity $\longrightarrow$ [____] $\longrightarrow$ Faster rate of [____] production

Reaction Time

REACTION TIME — [____]

Four steps to investigate reaction time:

1. Hold a [____] between the thumb and forefinger of the person being tested.

2. Drop the ruler without warning and [____]

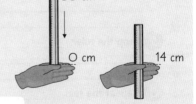

30 cm

0 cm   14 cm

3. [____] then calculate the mean distance that the ruler fell.

4. Repeat the experiment to investigate the effect of a factor on reaction time.

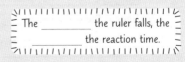

The [____] the ruler falls, the [____] the reaction time.

Required Practicals 4

Effect of Light Intensity on Photosynthesis Rate

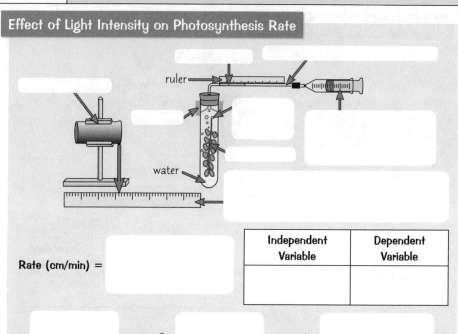

ruler

water

Rate (cm/min) =

Independent Variable	Dependent Variable

Reaction Time

REACTION TIME — .

Four steps to investigate reaction time:

1 Hold a ruler ....
....
....

2 Drop the ruler ....
....
....

3 Repeat the test ....
....
....

4 Repeat the experiment ....
....
....

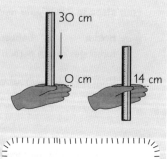

30 cm

O cm   14 cm

Required Practicals 5

Plant Growth Responses

You can investigate the effect of [_____] or [_____] on the growth of seedlings, e.g.:

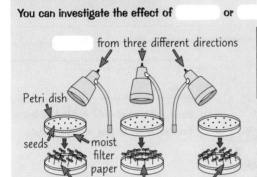

[_____] from three different directions

Petri dish

seeds — moist filter paper

seedlings grow [_____]

Independent Variable	Dependent Variable
direction of	direction of ....

Variables you should control to know the response is due to light only:

number and [_____] of seeds

[_____] temperature

light [_____]

Distribution and Abundance of Organisms

Four steps to estimate population size of small organisms using [_____]:

1 Place a 1 m² [_____] at random in a field.

2 [_____] all the daisies within it.

3 Repeat several times and work out the [_____]

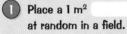

4 Multiply the [_____] by the number of [_____]

[_____] = total number of organisms

Three steps to find how organisms are distributed across an area using [_____] — e.g. distribution of daisies as you move away from the edge of a pond:

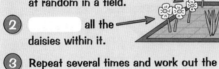

1 Mark out a line using a [_____].

2 Count the daisies in [_____] placed at regular [_____] along the line.

3 Draw a graph to show [_____]

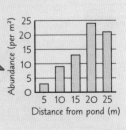

Abundance (per m²): 25, 20, 15, 10, 5, 0
Distance from pond (m): 5 10 15 20 25

Required Practicals 5

Plant Growth Responses

You can investigate the effect [   ] [   ], e.g.:

[   ]

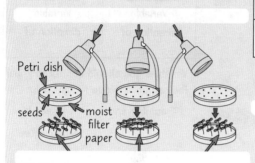

Petri dish

seeds — moist filter paper

Variables you should control to know the response is due to light only:

[   ]

[   ]   [   ]

[   ]

Distribution and Abundance of Organisms

Four steps to estimate [   ] of small organisms using [   ]:

 1 [   ]

2 [   ]

3 [   ]

mean = [   ]

4 [   ]

Three steps to find how organisms are [   ] using
[   ] — e.g. distribution of daisies as you move away from the edge of a pond:

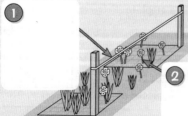

1 [   ]

3 Draw a graph to show how the daisies are [   ].

2 Count the [   ]

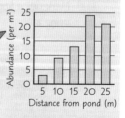

Abundance (per m²) — Distance from pond (m): 5 10 15 20 25

Required Practicals 6

Effect of Temperature on Rate of Decay

Six steps to investigate the effect of temperature on the rate of decay of _____ :

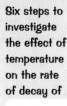
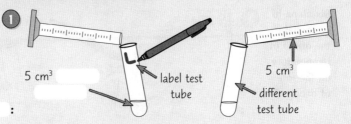

① 5 cm³ _____ _____   label test tube   5 cm³ _____   different test tube

② _____   add 5 drops of _____ to milk

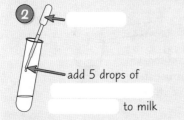

③ 7 cm³ sodium carbonate solution   milk solution becomes _____ (so turns _____)

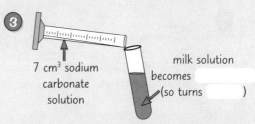

④ use a _____ to monitor temperature _____ at certain temperature

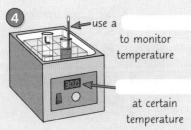

⑤ transfer 1 cm³ _____ solution to milk when solutions have reached water bath temperature

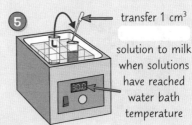

⑥ start a stopwatch immediately   stir with a glass rod   lipase _____ milk   milk _____, so no longer _____   stop the stopwatch

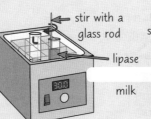

colour change from _____ to _____

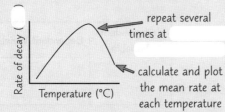

Rate of decay ( )   repeat several times at _____ _____   calculate and plot the mean rate at each temperature

Temperature (°C)

Independent Variable	Dependent Variable
	time taken for ....

Required Practicals 6

Effect of Temperature on Rate of Decay

Six steps to investigate the effect of temperature on the rate of decay of

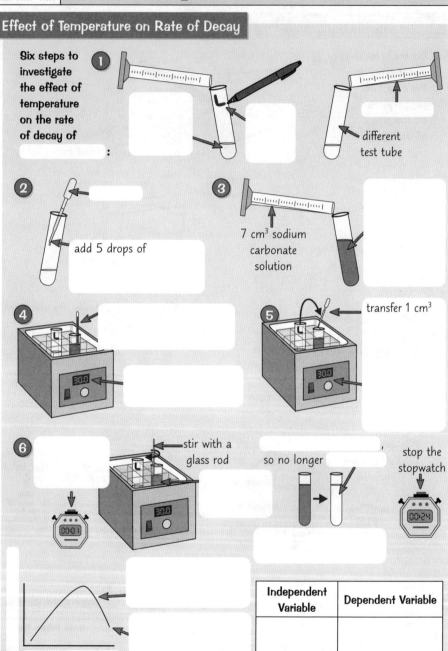

1.

different test tube

2.

add 5 drops of

3.

7 cm³ sodium carbonate solution

4.

5. transfer 1 cm³

6.

stir with a glass rod

so no longer

stop the stopwatch

Independent Variable	Dependent Variable

Mixed Practice Quizzes

It's less fun than actually doing the practicals, but it's quiz-time for pages 137-148.

Quiz 1   Date: ...... / ...... / ......

1) What does the coarse adjustment knob on a microscope do?
2) Why should a Petri dish containing an agar plate be stored upside down?
3) What is meant by 'reaction time'?
4) What is the independent variable when investigating how the time taken for amylase to break down starch changes with different pH buffers?
5) Which food molecule is biuret solution used to test for?
6) Explain why the mass of a potato cylinder might decrease after being left in a beaker of salt solution for 24 hours.
7) How can you vary light intensity to investigate its effect on photosynthesis?
8) Describe how you could test for the presence of lipids in a food sample.
9) If you're investigating the effect of light on the growth of seedlings, list three variables you should control.
10) How could you control temperature when investigating the decay of milk?

Total:

Quiz 2   Date: ...... / ...... / ......

1) Describe how to investigate the distribution of a plant along a transect.
2) How can pH be controlled when investigating its effect on amylase activity?
3) How could you tell if starch was present in a food sample?
4) How would you calculate the area of an inhibition zone?
5) What is measured when investigating temperature's effect on milk decay?
6) Describe how you could investigate the effect of light intensity on the rate of photosynthesis in pondweed.
7) How is the size of an inhibition zone related to an antibiotic's effectiveness?
8) Which knob do you use first when trying to focus a microscope image?
9) What does it mean if a food sample turns yellow after a Benedict's test?
10) True or false? When using quadrats to investigate population size in an area, the quadrats should be placed randomly.

Total:

Mixed Practice Quizzes

| Date: ...... / ...... / ......

1) If sugar is not present in a food sample, what will the sample look like following the Benedict's test?

2) List four things you should do when drawing a microscope image of cells.

3) In an investigation into osmosis, what should be done to potato cylinders removed from salt solution, before they are weighed?

4) How would you calculate the % change in mass of a potato cylinder?

5) How is an inoculating loop sterilised?

6) Describe how you could estimate the population size of a small organism in an area using quadrats.

7) What is an inhibition zone?

8) How can you tell when amylase has broken down all the starch in a solution?

9) What gas should you collect when investigating photosynthesis rate?

10) True or false? When using a microscope, use the lowest-powered lens first.

Total:

Quiz 4 | Date: ...... / ...... / ......

1) A positive result of which food test involves a colour change to purple?

2) Describe how you could investigate a person's reaction time using a ruler.

3) Describe one way you could investigate the effect of light on plant growth.

4) At what temperature should a Petri dish containing bacteria be stored?

5) What is the dependent variable when investigating how light direction affects plant growth?

6) Why are Petri dishes sterilised before being used to grow bacteria?

7) How can microorganisms in the air be kept from getting into a Petri dish?

8) How do you work out the rate at which amylase breaks down starch in s^{-1}?

9) What enzyme and foodstuff could you use when investigating the effect of temperature on rate of decay?

10) Describe how you could investigate the effectiveness of different antibiotics on bacterial growth.

Total:

Measuring and Sampling

Taking Measurements

Mass

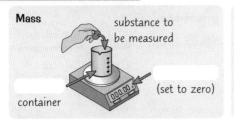

substance to
be measured

(set to zero)

container

Temperature

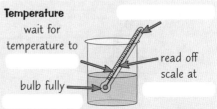

wait for
temperature to

read off
scale at

bulb fully

Volume of a liquid — three methods

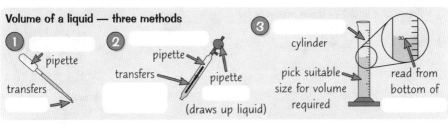

1 pipette

transfers

2 pipette

transfers

pipette

(draws up liquid)

3 cylinder

pick suitable
size for volume
required

read from
bottom of

30

Volume of a gas

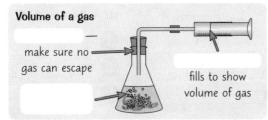

—

make sure no
gas can escape

fills to show
volume of gas

pH — three methods

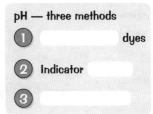

1   dyes

2 Indicator

3

Sampling

It's generally not possible to

in a population, so you usually need to

take a   to represent the population.

If a sample doesn't

as a whole, it's said to
be

Assign a number to
of the population.

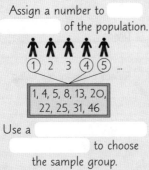

① 2 3 ④ ⑤ ...

1, 4, 5, 8, 13, 20,
22, 25, 31, 46

Use a

to choose
the sample group.

To choose sample sites from a   :

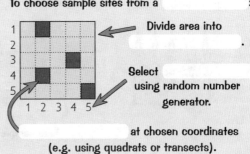

Divide area into

Select
using random number
generator.

at chosen coordinates
(e.g. using quadrats or transects).

Second Go:
...... / ...... / ......

Measuring and Sampling

Taking Measurements

Mass

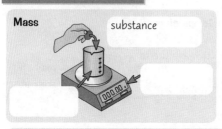

substance

Temperature

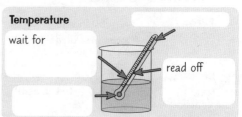

wait for

read off

Volume of a liquid — three methods

 ....

pipette

pipette

transfers

....

....

....

3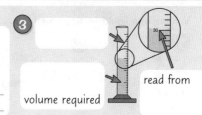

volume required

read from

Volume of a gas

airtight —

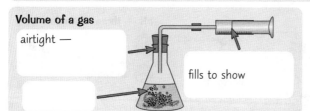

fills to show

pH — three methods

1

2

3

Sampling

It's generally not possible to

If a sample ....
....
....
....

Assign a number to

To choose .... :

① 2 3 ④ ⑤ ...

1, 4, 5, 8, 13, 20,
22, 25, 31, 46

Use a

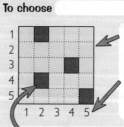

Divide ....
....

Select coordinates using
....
....

Take samples at

Practical Skills

Practical Techniques

Heating

Bunsen burners

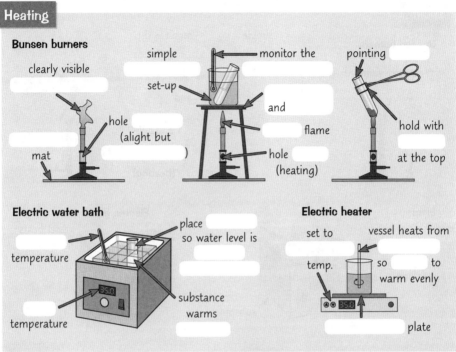

clearly visible

simple

set-up

monitor the

pointing

hole
(alight but   )

and

flame

hold with

mat

hole
(heating)

at the top

Electric water bath

place
so water level is

temperature

substance
warms

temperature

Electric heater

set to

vessel heats from

temp.

so   to
warm evenly

plate

Safety

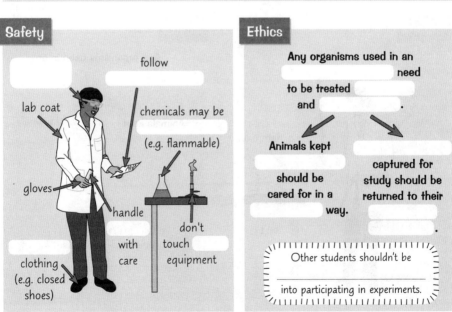

follow

lab coat

chemicals may be

(e.g. flammable)

gloves

handle

don't
touch
equipment

with
care

clothing
(e.g. closed
shoes)

Ethics

Any organisms used in an
need
to be treated
and   .

Animals kept

should be
cared for in a
way.

captured for
study should be
returned to their

Other students shouldn't be

into participating in experiments.

Practical Skills

Practical Techniques

Heating

Bunsen burners

clearly visible

mat

simple

_____

_____

monitor the

_____

and _____

_____ flame

_____ (heating)

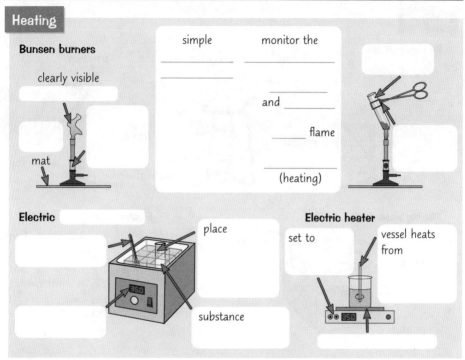

Electric _____

place

substance

Electric heater

set to

vessel heats from

Safety

(e.g. flammable)

don't

with care

(e.g. closed shoes)

Ethics

Any organisms used in an

Animals kept   **Wild animals**

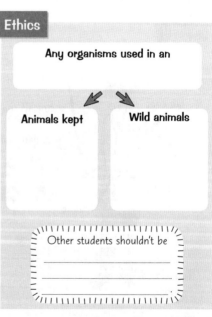

Other students shouldn't be

_____

_____

Practical Skills

 ☑   ☑   ☑

Techniques and Results

Five Steps to Measure Rate of Water Uptake

1. Assemble the potometer [_____].

2. Cut the shoot at a [_____] underwater and insert it in the [_____].

3. Remove the apparatus [_____], keeping the [_____] submerged in the beaker.

4. Remove the [_____] from the beaker of water until [_____], then put it back in the beaker.

5. As the plant [_____], it takes up water, so the bubble [_____].

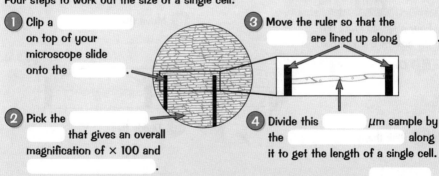

of water

water

tap

during experiment

movement

with a scale

beaker of water

Cell Size and Scale Bars

Four steps to work out the size of a single cell:

1. Clip a [_____] on top of your microscope slide onto the [_____].

2. Pick the [_____] that gives an overall magnification of × 100 and [_____].

3. Move the ruler so that the [_____] are lined up along [_____].

4. Divide this [_____] µm sample by the [_____] along it to get the length of a single cell.

of cell

$$[\_\_\_\_] \ \text{length} = \frac{\text{drawn cell length} \ [\_\_\_\_] \ \text{length represented by scale bar}}{\text{actual cell length}}$$

100 µm

Percentage Change

To compare results that didn't have the [_____], calculate the percentage change:

$$\% \ \text{change} = \frac{[\_\_\_\_] \ \text{value} - [\_\_\_\_] \ \text{value}}{\text{original value}} \times 100$$

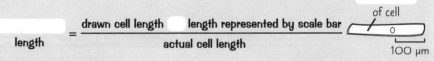

Practical Skills

Techniques and Results

Five Steps to Measure Rate of Water Uptake

1 Assemble the ....

2 Cut the ....
and insert ....

3 Remove the apparatus from the water,
....
....

4 Remove the capillary tube from the
....
....
....

5 As the plant ....
....
....

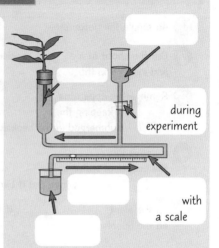

during experiment

with a scale

Cell Size and Scale Bars

Four steps to work out
the size of a single cell:

1 Clip a

3 Move the

2 Pick the

4 Divide this

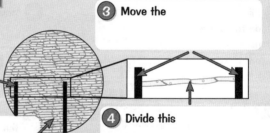

= ──────── length × length represented by scale bar

100 μm

Percentage Change

To compare results that didn't have
the same

%
change = ────────────── ×
        value

Mixed Practice Quizzes

All clued up on your practical skills? Good — then you'll have no problem answering these questions from p.151-156. Take them on one quiz at a time.

Quiz 1 — Date: ...... / ...... / ......

1) What is a biased sample?
2) Why might you need to use percentage change to compare your results?
3) What colour is the flame of a Bunsen burner with the hole open?
4) Give three methods for measuring pH.
5) What is a potometer used to measure?
6) How do you use an electric heater?
7) Give a piece of equipment that can be used to measure the volume of a gas.
8) What is a meniscus?
9) True or false? When using an electric water bath, the level of the substance you're heating should be above that of the water in the bath.
10) Why are random samples usually studied instead of whole populations?

Total:

Quiz 2 — Date: ...... / ...... / ......

1) Describe how to use a potometer to measure rate of water uptake.
2) What piece of equipment is used to measure temperature?
3) When a Bunsen burner is not being used for heating, should the hole be open or closed?
4) Describe how to use an electric water bath.
5) Describe how to choose random sample sites from a large area.
6) True or false? Balances should never be set to zero.
7) What is a scale bar used for on a microscopy drawing of cells?
8) Name a type of pipette that can be used to transfer accurate volumes.
9) Give three items of safety equipment used in a lab.
10) True or false? Wild animals captured for study should not be returned to their original habitat.

Total:

Mixed Practice Quizzes

Quiz 3   Date: ...... / ...... / ......

1) How should any organisms used in an investigation be treated?
2) What piece of equipment is used to measure mass?
3) What should a Bunsen burner be placed on?
4) Give three methods of heating a substance in a lab.
5) True or false? The bulb of a thermometer must be fully submerged when measuring the temperature of a liquid.
6) Why do you need to stir the substance you're heating when using an electric heater?
7) Describe how a shoot should be cut before it is inserted in a potometer.
8) Why must your equipment be airtight when measuring the volume of gas?
9) Describe how to take a random sample from a population of people.
10) What can you use to hold a boiling tube over a Bunsen burner flame?

Total:

Quiz 4   Date: ...... / ...... / ......

1) Give two pieces of equipment used to measure the volume of liquids.
2) When measuring water uptake, what happens to the bubble in the potometer as the plant transpires?
3) Give the equation for percentage change.
4) Describe how to set up a simple water bath using a Bunsen burner.
5) True or false? The volume of liquid in a measuring cylinder should be read from the bottom of the meniscus.
6) When heating a substance in a boiling tube, how should the tube be angled to ensure it is being heated safely?
7) Give three potential hazards found in a lab.
8) Describe how to measure the temperature of a liquid.
9) If a Bunsen burner flame is yellow, is the hole open or closed?
10) Describe how to measure the length of a cell using a microscope.

Total: